CASAS TEST PREP
STUDENT BOOK FOR MATH GOALS
FORM 913M LEVEL A/B

*Preparing Adult Students
for CASAS Math GOALS Tests
and for Workforce Entrance Math Exams*

COACHING FOR BETTER LEARNING, LLC

Copyright © 2019 Coaching For Better Learning, LLC
All rights reserved
ISBN: 978-1-6774-1661-5

TABLE OF CONTENT

	Introduction	Page 6
Chapter 1	Number and Operations: Base Ten	Page 8
Chapter 2	Fraction and Ratios	Page 27
Chapter 3	Algebra Thinking	Page 34
Chapter 4	Geometry	Page 44
Chapter 5	Measurement and Data	Page 56
Chapter 6	Data Analysis	Page 69
Chapter 7	Practice Tests	Page 77
	Practice Test 1	Page 78
	Practice Test 2	Page 88
	Answer Keys	Page 98

INTRODUCTION

This CASAS Test Prep student math textbook is designed to help teachers prepare adult students for the CASAS Math GOALS Test Form 913M Level A/B and for workforce and vocational training entrance math tests.

The content of this textbook is aligned with CASAS Competencies, with College and Career Readiness (CCR) and National Reporting System (NRS) standards and follows the CASAS GOALS Math Form 913M test blueprint.

In other words, this math textbook presents learning activities that help adult education programs, workforce programs, and their adult students to meet the Workforce Innovation and Opportunity Act (WIOA) math expectations.

This CASAS test prep textbook offers

- Seven (7) main chapters that cover NRS, CASAS and CCR standards and content such as

    o **Number and Operations: Base Ten**
    o **Fraction and Ratios**
    o **Algebra Thinking**
    o **Geometry**
    o **Measurement and Data**
    o **Data Analysis**
    o **Practice Tests and Answer Keys**

- Step-by-step instruction, plus practice exercises and answer keys

- Questions and tasks that encourage pair work, group work, and classroom discussion on math ideas and concepts

- Real world word problems and key concepts

- Two (2) practice tests that mimic the CASAS Math GOALS Form 913M test format and rigor, plus answer keys

Specifically, this textbook allows math teachers to provide learners with the space and time to experiment with math concepts and ideas and to get deeper in their learning process. For example, the tasks presented in this book aim to

- Make learners think more deeply about math structure and concepts and therefore improve their mathematical thinking skills
- Provide learners with hands-on tasks relevant to their situation
- Help learners connect their math learning with the real world
- Create opportunities for learners to read about, write about, and discuss math ideas and concepts
- Invite learners to reflect on their learning

Therefore, we encourage math teachers and students to NOT use this textbook as a collection of worksheets to use in isolation. Rather, for effective use of this resource, we highly recommended that learners have a safe classroom environment where they can collaborate with their classmates in pairs or in groups.

The use will be more productive if students are in a learner-centered classroom where they can learn to appreciate the beauty of math, experiment with math ideas, make mistakes and take risks, discuss their work and methods, and articulate their understanding of math ideas and concepts without the fear of being judged.

In a nutshell, this CASAS Test prep math textbook covers more than the basic content that learners need to master so they can perform very well on the CASAS Math GOALS Form 913M test.

Now that you know what's in the textbook, let's get to work. Enjoy the journey!

CHAPTER 1

NUMBER AND OPERATIONS: BASE TEN

Key Vocabulary

place value, multi-digit whole numbers, decimal numbers, odd numbers, even numbers, fractions, mixed numbers, proportions, ratios

Place value

In our decimal number system, the value of a **digit** depends on its place, or position, in a number. Each place has a value that is **10 times** the place to its right. Multi-digit numbers in their standard form are separated into groups of three digits using commas. In other words, each digit represents a different **place value**.

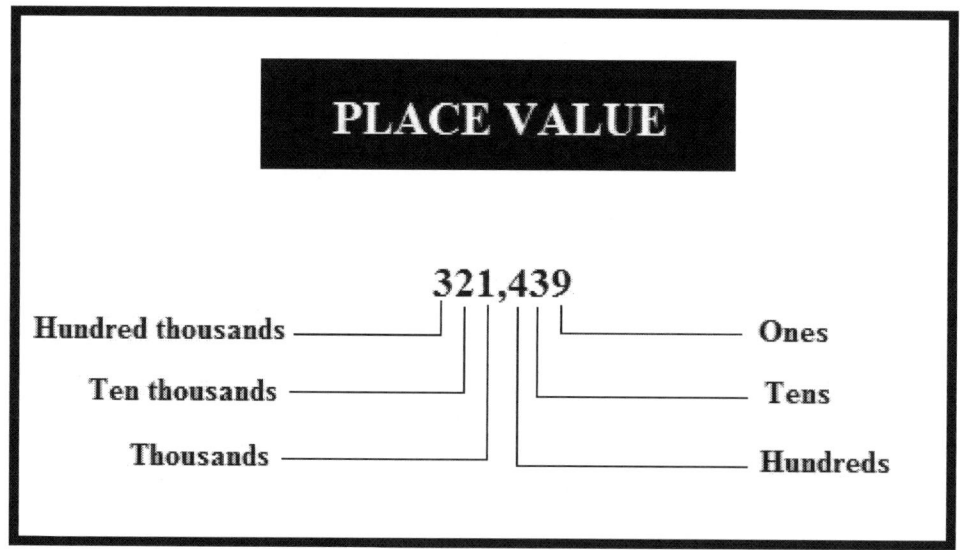

Example: What does the 8 mean in the number 5,876?

Step 1. Notice that 8 represents the hundreds place.

Step 2. Thus, the number 8 means **8 hundreds.**

Writing out a number using the place value (ones, tens, and so on) is called **expanded form**.

Example: Write 9,843 in expanded form.

Step 1. The first digit (9) is the thousands' place. It means there are 9 thousands in the number 9,843.

Step 2. The second digit (8) is the hundreds' place. It means there are 8 hundreds in the number 9,843.

Step 3. The third digit (4) is the tens' place. It means that there are 4 tens in the number 9,843.

Step 4. The last digit (3) is the ones' place. It means that there are 3 ones in the number 9,843.

Step 5. Thus, the number 9,843 can be written as follows:

9 thousands, 8 hundreds, 4 tens, and 3 ones

Notice that this number can also be written as follows:

$$9,843 = 9000 + 800 + 40 + 3$$

To write a number in **words**, first break down the number in expanded form, then combine the values into a number sentence.

Example: Write the number 7,549 in words.

Step 1. According to the place value, the first digit (7) is in the thousands' place. This means there are **seven thousands** in the number 7,549.

Step 2. The second digit (5) is the hundreds' place. This means there are **five hundreds** in the number 7,549.

Step 3. The third digit (4) is the tens' place. This means there are **four tens** in the number 7,549.

Step 4. The last digit (9) is the ones' place. This means there are **nine ones** in the number 7,549.

Step 5. Thus, the number 7,549 in words is

Seven thousand five hundred forty-nine

Addition and subtraction of numbers

To add and subtract numbers, we must line up the numbers vertically by matching the **place values**, starting with the ones' place.

Example: Paul wrote 593 hit songs that made it on the best-seller charts. Something many people don't know, however, is that he also wrote 38 songs that were never released. How many songs did Paul write in all?

Step 1. Note that we must add the numbers. Line up the numbers vertically by matching the place values.

$$\begin{array}{r} 593\ + \\ \underline{38} \end{array}$$

Step 2. Add the ones column: 3 + 8 = 11. Now we can put the 1 ten from 11 with the tens and write "1" in the ones' place.

$$\begin{array}{r} 1 \\ 593\ + \\ \underline{38} \\ 1 \end{array}$$

Step 3. Add the tens, including the 1 ten that was regrouped to the tens column: 9 + 3 + 1 = 13

$$\begin{array}{r} 1 \\ 593\ + \\ \underline{38} \\ 31 \end{array}$$

Step 4. Add the hundreds, including the 1 hundred that was regrouped: 5 + 1 = 6

$$\begin{array}{r} 593\ + \\ \underline{38} \\ 631 \end{array}$$

Step 5. Thus, Paul wrote **631 songs.**

Example: Find the difference: 550 – 28

Step 1. To find the difference, subtract 28 from 550. Line up the numbers vertically by matching the place values.

$$\begin{array}{r} 550\,- \\ 28 \\ \hline \end{array}$$

Step 2. We must exchange **1 ten** from the tens' column in 550 and give it to the zero in the ones' column to make the number **10**. Ten is larger than 8, which is large enough to be subtracted from.

$$\begin{array}{r} 10 \\ 550\,- \\ 28 \\ \hline \end{array}$$

Step 3. Subtract 10 – 8 to get 2

$$\begin{array}{r} 10 \\ 550\,- \\ 28 \\ \hline 2 \end{array}$$

Step 4. When we exchanged 1 ten from the tens column in 550, the number 5 became 4

$$\begin{array}{r} 4 \\ 550\,- \\ 28 \\ \hline 2 \end{array}$$

Step 5. Subtract 4 – 2 and put "5" in the hundreds column.

$$\begin{array}{r} 4 \\ 550\,- \\ 28 \\ \hline 522 \end{array}$$

Step 5. Thus, the difference is **522**

When adding and subtracting multi-digit whole numbers, digits are aligned according to place value, and the computation is performed from right to left.

Example: Add 9,378 + 946

Step 1. To add multi-digit whole numbers, align the digits according to place value, then perform the computation from right to left.

$$\begin{array}{r} 9,378\, + \\ 946 \\ \hline \end{array}$$

Step 2. Add the ones: 8 + 6 = 14

$$\begin{array}{r} 1 \\ 9,378\, + \\ 946 \\ \hline 4 \end{array}$$

Step 3. Add the tens, including the 1 ten that was regrouped: 7 + 4 + 1 = 12

$$\begin{array}{r} 1\,1 \\ 9,378\, + \\ 946 \\ \hline 24 \end{array}$$

Step 4. Add the hundreds, including the 1 hundred that was regrouped: 3 + 9 + 1 = 13

$$\begin{array}{r} 1\,1\,1 \\ 9,378\, + \\ 946 \\ \hline 324 \end{array}$$

Step 5. Add the thousands, including the 1 thousand that was regrouped: 9 + 1 = 10

$$\begin{array}{r} 1\,1\,1 \\ 9,378\, + \\ 946 \\ \hline 10,324 \end{array}$$

Step 6. Thus, 9,378 + 946 = **10,324**

Decimal numbers

Numbers expressed in decimal form are called decimal numbers or **decimals**. A decimal has two parts: the whole number part and the decimal part. These parts are separated by a dot (**.**) called the **decimal point.**

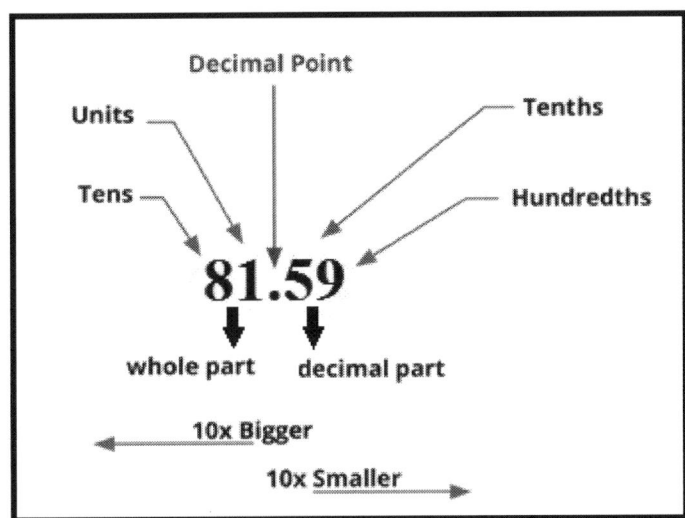

When adding and subtracting decimals, add or subtract as normal, but make sure to keep **the decimal points aligned.**

Example: Add 15.86 + 8.32

Step 1. Keep the decimal points aligned and draw a line.

$$15.86 + \\ \underline{8.32}$$

Step 2. Add the numbers as whole numbers.

$$\begin{array}{r} 1\ 1 \\ 15.86 + \\ \underline{8.32} \\ 24.18 \end{array}$$

Step 3. Thus, 15.86 + 8.32 = **24.18**

Example: There were 12.54 gallons of water in Kevin's bathtub. Then 3.18 gallons drained out. How much water is left in the bathtub?

Step 1. Notice that this problem requires subtraction of decimal numbers.

Step 2. Subtract the numbers of gallons. Remember to line up the decimal points.

$$\begin{array}{r} 12.54 - \\ \underline{3.18} \\ 9.36 \end{array}$$

Step 3. Thus, **9.36 gallons** of water are left.

Even and odd numbers

Any integer that can be divided exactly by 2 is an **even number**. The last digit of an even number is 0, 2, 4, 6, or 8.
    Any integer that **cannot** be divided exactly by 2 is an **odd number**. The last digit of an odd number is 1, 3, 5, 7, or 9.

Example: Which one of the following is odd?

34, 70, 17, 98

Step 1. Notice that the last digit of 17 is 7, and the other numbers are even.

Step 2. Thus, **17** is the odd number.

Example: Which one of the following is even?

233, 501, 499, 770

Step 1. Notice that the las digit of 770 is 0, and the other numbers are odd.

Step 2. Thus, **770** is the even number.

Fractions

A **fraction** is a number that represents a whole number that has been divided into equal parts. For example, if we have a circle and we divide it into 6 equal slices, 1 of those slices is written as 1/6, as shown here:

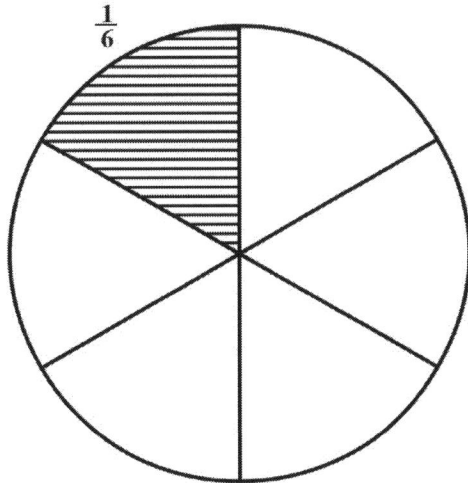

A fraction is made up of two parts: the denominator and the numerator.

The **denominator** is the bottom number of the fraction. It is the number of parts the whole is divided into.

The **numerator** is the top number of the fraction. It is the number of parts we have.

$$\frac{1}{6} \begin{array}{l} \rightarrow \textbf{Numerator} \\ \rightarrow \textbf{Denominator} \end{array}$$

Example: What fraction of the shape is dark?

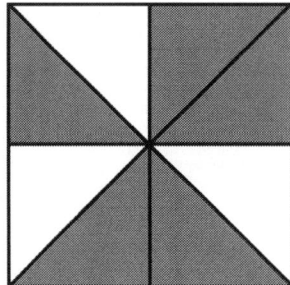

Step 1. Notice that the shape is divided into 8 equal parts. Thus, the denominator is 8.

Step 2. Notice that the gray area is formed by 5 equal parts. Thus, the numerator is 5.

Step 3. Thus, the fraction is $\frac{5}{8}$

Mixed numbers

A mixed number is a whole number and a proper fraction combined. For example, $4\frac{2}{5}$ is a mixed number.

We can use either an improper fraction or a mixed fraction to show the same amount. An improper fraction is a fraction where the numerator is greater than or equal to the denominator. To convert an improper fraction to a mixed number, follow these steps:

1. Divide the numerator by the denominator.
2. Write down the whole number answer.
3. Write down any remainder above the denominator.

Example: Convert $\frac{5}{4}$ to a mixed number.

Step 1. Divide 5 by 4.

$$5 \div 4 = 1 \text{ with remainder of } 1$$

Step 2. Write down the 1. Then write down the remainder (1) above the denominator (4).

$$1\frac{1}{4}$$

Step 3. Thus, we get:

$$\frac{5}{4} = 1\frac{1}{4}$$

To convert a mixed number to an improper fraction, follow these steps:

1. Multiply the whole number part by the fraction's denominator.
2. Add the result to the numerator.
3. Then write the result on top of the denominator.

Example: Convert $2\frac{3}{5}$ to an improper fraction.

Step 1. Multiply the whole number part by the denominator: 2 x 5 = 10

Step 2. Add the result to the numerator: 10 + 3 = 13

Step 3. Write that result above the denominator.

$$\frac{13}{5}$$

Step 4. Thus, we get:

$$2\frac{3}{5} = \frac{13}{5}$$

Multiplication and division of fractions

To multiply fractions, multiply the numerators of the fractions to get the new numerator, and multiply the denominators of the fractions to get the new denominator.

Example: Multiply $\frac{3}{4}$ x $\frac{5}{7}$

Step 1. Multiply the numerators and the denominators of the fractions to get the result.

$$\frac{3}{4} \times \frac{5}{7} = \frac{15}{28}$$

To multiply fractions by whole numbers, we can rewrite whole numbers as fractions. Then we multiply the numerators and denominators of the fractions.

Example: Multiply $4 \times \frac{3}{5}$

Step 1. Rewrite the whole number as a fraction. To rewrite a whole number as a fraction, simply place the whole number over 1.

$$\frac{4}{1} \times \frac{3}{5}$$

Step 2. Multiply the numerators and the denominators of the fractions.

$$\frac{4}{1} \times \frac{3}{5} = \frac{12}{5}$$

Step 3. Thus, we get:

$$4 \times \frac{3}{5} = \frac{12}{5}$$

To divide fractions, follow these steps:

1. Turn the second fraction upside down. (This is now a **reciprocal**.)
2. Multiply the first fraction by that reciprocal.
3. Simplify the fraction (if needed).

Example: Divide $\frac{2}{3} \div \frac{3}{7}$

Step 1. Turn the second fraction upside down. (It becomes a **reciprocal**.)

$$\frac{3}{7} \text{ becomes } \frac{7}{3}$$

Step 2. Multiply the first fraction by that **reciprocal**.

$$\frac{2}{3} \times \frac{7}{3} = \frac{14}{9}$$

Step 3. Thus,

$$\frac{2}{3} \div \frac{3}{7} = \frac{14}{9}$$

We can solve problems when they require multiplying and/or dividing with fractions and mixed numbers.

Example: A piece of land is $3\frac{3}{4}$ miles wide. It is 5 times as long as it is wide. How long is the piece of land?

Step 1. Multiply $3\frac{3}{4} \times 5$

Step 2. Write $3\frac{3}{4}$ as an improper fraction.

$$3\frac{3}{4} = \frac{(3 \cdot 4) + 3}{4}$$

$$3\frac{3}{4} = \frac{12 + 3}{4} = \frac{15}{4}$$

Step 3. Then multiply $\frac{15}{4} \times 5$

$$\frac{15}{4} \times 5 = \frac{15}{4} \times \frac{5}{1}$$

$$\frac{15}{4} \times 5 = \frac{75}{4}$$

Step 4. Write $\frac{75}{4}$ as a mixed number.

$$\frac{75}{4} = 18\frac{3}{4}$$

Step 5. The length of the piece of land is $\mathbf{18\frac{3}{4}}$ **miles**.

Multiply and divide multi-digit integers and decimal numbers

Example: Multiply 532 x 36

Step 1. Write the multiplier under the multiplicand and draw a line.

$$\begin{array}{r} 532 \times \\ \underline{36} \end{array}$$

Step 2. Multiply the multiplicand by each digit of the multiplier. Place the ones digit of each partial product in the same column as the multiplying digit.

$$\begin{array}{r} 11 \\ 532 \times \\ \underline{36} \\ 3192 \\ 1596 \end{array}$$

Step 3. Add the partial products.

$$\begin{array}{r} 11 \\ 532 \times \\ \underline{36} \\ 3192\ + \\ \underline{1596} \\ 19{,}152 \end{array}$$

Example: Divide 3,193 ÷ 5

Step 1. Rewrite the problem to set it up for long division.

$$5\,\overline{)3193}$$

Step 2. Divide the first digit of the dividend, 3, by the divisor, 5.

$$5\,\overline{)3193}$$

Step 3. Since 5 does not go into 3, we must use the first *two* digits of the dividend and divide 31 by 5. The divisor, 5, goes into 31 six times. We write the 6 in the quotient above the 1.

$$\begin{array}{r} 6 \\ 5\overline{)3193} \end{array}$$

Step 4. Multiply the 6 in the quotient by the divisor, 5, and write the product, 30, under the first two digits in the dividend.

$$\begin{array}{r} 6 \\ 5\overline{)3193} \\ 30 \end{array}$$

Step 5. Subtract that product from the first two digits in the dividend. So, subtract 31 − 30. Write the difference, 1, under the second digit in the dividend.

$$\begin{array}{r} 6 \\ 5\overline{)3193} \\ \underline{30} \\ 1 \end{array}$$

Step 6. Now bring down the 9 and repeat these steps for the 19. There are 3 fives in 19. Write the 3 over the 9. Multiply the 3 by 5 and subtract the product (15) from 19.

$$\begin{array}{r} 63 \\ 5\overline{)3193} \\ \underline{30} \\ 19 \\ \underline{15} \\ 4 \end{array}$$

Step 7. Bring down the 3 and repeat these steps for the 43. There are 8 fives in 43. Write the 8 over the 3. Multiply the 8 by 5 and subtract this product (40) from 43.

$$\begin{array}{r} \mathbf{638} \\ 5\overline{)3193} \\ \underline{30} \\ 19 \\ \underline{15} \\ 43 \\ \underline{40} \\ 3 \end{array} \longrightarrow \text{Remainder}$$

We can check our answer by multiplying, and then adding the remainder.

$$(638 \times 5) + 3 = 3{,}193$$

To multiply decimals, ignore the decimal points (that is, do not align them) and multiply the numbers as whole numbers. Then place the decimal point. Starting from the right of the product, separate as many decimal digits as there are in the two numbers total.

Example: Multiply 6.3 x 4.75

Step 1. Ignore the decimal points and multiply the numbers as whole numbers.

$$63 \times 475 = 29925$$

Step 2. Now we must place the decimal point. Notice that 6.3 and 4.75 together have three decimal digits. Thus, the product will have three decimal digits.

$$29.925$$

Step 3. Thus, 6.3 x 4.75 = **29.925**

To divide a decimal by another decimal number, we can keep multiplying both the dividend and the divisor by 10 until the divisor becomes a whole number.

Example: Divide 35.7 ÷ 1.02

Step 1. Multiply both numbers in the problem by 10 until the divisor is a whole number.

$$35.7 \div 1.02 \quad \text{(original problem)}$$
$$357 \div 10.2 \quad \text{(multiply by 10)}$$
$$3{,}570 \div 102 \quad \text{(multiply by 10; now the divisor is a whole number)}$$

Step 2. The last problem, 3,570 ÷ 102, is equivalent to the original problem and easy to solve. The answer is 35.

Step 3. Thus, 35.7 ÷ 1.02 = **35**

We can solve problems when it requires multiplying and/or dividing with multi-digit positive integers and decimal numbers.

Example: Jessica's dog eats 1.125 pounds of dog food each day. How much dog food will Jessica's dog eat in 5 weeks?

Step 1. First, convert 5 weeks to days.

$$5 \text{ weeks} = 5 \times 7 \text{ days} = 35 \text{ days}$$

Step 2. Multiply 1.125 x 35

$$1.125 \times 35 = 39.375$$

Step 3. Jessica's dog will eat **39.375 pounds** of dog food in 5 weeks.

Proportions

A proportion is a name we give to a statement in which two ratios are equal. It can be written as follows:

$$\frac{a}{b} = \frac{c}{d}$$

When two ratios are equal, the cross products of the ratios are equal.

$$\frac{a}{b} = \frac{c}{d}$$

$$a \cdot d = b.c$$

Example: Paul earned $42 in 3 hours at his job today. He wants to know how much he could earn tomorrow if he works 8 hours at the same hourly rate.

Step 1. Let *x* be the amount of money that Paul could earn.

Step 2. Write the proportion that represents the problem.

$$\frac{\$42}{3\ hr} = \frac{x}{8\ hr}$$

Step 3. Apply the cross product.

$$\frac{\$42}{3\ hr} = \frac{x}{8\ hr}$$

$$3hr \cdot x = \$42 \cdot 8\ hr$$

Step 4. Solve the equation.

$$3hr \cdot x = \$42 \cdot 8\,hr$$

$$x = \frac{\$42 \cdot 8hr}{3hr} = \$112$$

Step 5. Paul could earn **$112** tomorrow.

Practice Exercises

1) A 4-digit number has a 9 in the thousands place, a 5 in the ones place, and 0s elsewhere. What is the number?

   A. 5,009
   B. 9,500
   C. 9,050
   D. 9,005

2) What is another way to show 564?

   A. 500 x 64
   B. 500 + 60 + 40
   C. 500 + 60 + 4
   D. 5 + 60 + 400

3) The school library bought 572 new books last year. They bought 469 new books this year. How many new books did they buy altogether?

   A. 1,041
   B. 941
   C. 1,031
   D. 871

4) On Saturday, Harry's Supermarket sold 268 pounds of ground beef. On Sunday they sold twice that amount. On Monday they only sold 177 pounds. How much more meat did they sell on Sunday than Monday?

   A. 536
   B. 713
   C. 359
   D. 91

5) Which of the following operations is equal to an even number?

   A. 3 x 7
   B. 8 + 15
   C. 20 + 22
   D. 10 − 5

6) Which of the following is an odd number?

   A. 990
   B. 1,001
   C. 78
   D. 444

7) It rained 2.19 inches on Tuesday. On Wednesday, it rained 0.76 inches less than on Tuesday. How much did it rain on Wednesday?

   A. 1.43
   B. 0.43
   C. 1.33
   D. 2.95

8) A sandwich shop employee named Peter takes 7.6 minutes to make a sandwich. How long does it take him to make 24 sandwiches?

   A. 18.24 minutes
   B. 1 hour and 24 minutes
   C. 182.4 minutes
   D. 456 seconds

9) There was $\frac{2}{3}$ of a pie left in the fridge. Daniel ate $\frac{2}{5}$ of the leftover pie. How much of a pie did he leave?

   A. $\frac{4}{15}$
   B. $\frac{10}{6}$
   C. $\frac{4}{8}$
   D. $\frac{1}{2}$

10) A track coach wants his athletes to race $\frac{7}{2}$ miles around a track to measure how fast each person can run. If the track is $\frac{1}{2}$ mile around, how many laps around the track will the athletes have to run to complete the race?

    A. 2
    B. 3
    C. 5
    D. 7

11) Add 2.34 + 5.98

    A. 8.22
    B. 7.92
    C. 8.32
    D. 6.79

12) Which of the following is a mixed number?

    A. 0.675
    B. 2,561
    C. $\frac{7}{9}$
    D. $12\frac{1}{4}$

13) Subtract 2,020 – 348

    A. 1,592
    B. 1,672
    C. 2,348
    D. 1,882

14) Multiply 6,942 x 57

    A. 395,694
    B. 278,934
    C. 403,014
    D. 388,544

15) Divide 1,000 ÷ 25

    A. 45
    B. 50
    C. 25
    D. 40

Answer Key

1) D   2) C   3) A   4) C   5) C   6) B   7) A   8) C   9) A   10) D   11) C   12) D   13) B   14) A   15) D

Reflection on learning

Answer the following reflection questions and feel free to discuss your responses with your teacher or a classmate.

1- What math idea, principle, or structure did you learn from this section?

2- What math concepts did you learn?

3- What procedures or method did you work on in this section?

4- What aspect of this section is still not 100% clear for you?

5- What else do you want your teacher to know?

CHAPTER 2

FRACTIONS AND RATIOS

Key Vocabulary

> fractions, whole numbers, multiplication, division, ratio, numerator, denominator, integer

Fractions

We know a **fraction** is a number that represents a whole number that has been divided into equal parts. Whole numbers can be represented as fractions. For example, 6 can be written as follows:

$$6 = \frac{12}{2}$$

In other words, a fraction represents a division of two integers.

To add and subtract fractions with whole numbers, we can convert the whole number to a fraction.

Example: Add $3 + \frac{2}{5}$

Step 1. Convert 3 to a fraction where the denominator is equal to 5 since the denominator in $\frac{2}{5}$ is 5

$$3 = \frac{15}{5}$$

Step 2. Add $\frac{15}{5} + \frac{2}{5}$

Step 3. Since the fractions have the same denominator, add the numerators and keep the same denominator.

$$\frac{15}{5} + \frac{2}{5} = \frac{15+2}{5} = \frac{17}{5}$$

Step 4. Thus, $3 + \frac{2}{5} = \frac{17}{5}$

Example: Subtract $1 - \frac{2}{7}$

Step 1. Convert 1 to a fraction where the denominator is equal to 7

$$1 = \frac{7}{7}$$

Step 2. Subtract $\frac{7}{7} - \frac{2}{7}$

Step 3. Since the fractions have the same denominator, subtract the numerators and keep the same denominator.

$$\frac{7}{7} - \frac{2}{7} = \frac{7-2}{7} = \frac{5}{7}$$

Step 4. Thus, $1 - \frac{2}{7} = \frac{5}{7}$

To multiply fractions by whole numbers, rewrite whole numbers as fractions. Then multiply the numerators and denominators of the fractions.

Example: Multiply $6 \: x \: \frac{5}{2}$

Step 1. Rewrite the whole number as a fraction. To rewrite a whole number as a fraction, simply place the whole number over 1.

$$\frac{6}{1} \: x \: \frac{5}{2}$$

Step 2. Multiply the numerators and the denominators of the fractions.

$$\frac{6}{1} \times \frac{5}{2} = \frac{30}{2}$$

Step 3. We can interpret a fraction as **the division of the numerator by the denominator**. In other words, divide the numerator by the denominator.

$$\frac{30}{2} = 15$$

Step 4. Thus, we get

$$6 \times \frac{5}{2} = \mathbf{15}$$

To divide fractions by whole numbers, rewrite whole numbers as fractions. Then multiply the first fraction by the **reciprocal of the second fraction**.

Example: Divide $8 \div \frac{3}{4}$

Step 1. Rewrite the whole number as a fraction. To rewrite a whole number as a fraction, simply place the whole number over 1.

$$\frac{8}{1} \div \frac{3}{4}$$

Step 2. Multiply the first fraction by the reciprocal of the second fraction.

$$\frac{8}{1} \times \frac{4}{3} = \frac{32}{3}$$

Step 3. Thus, we get

$$8 \div \frac{3}{4} = \frac{32}{3}$$

Practice Exercises

1) The number 8 can be written as:

A. $\frac{1}{8}$

B. $\frac{8}{2}$

C. $\frac{24}{3}$

D. $\frac{16}{3}$

2) Which of the following sums represents the following figure?

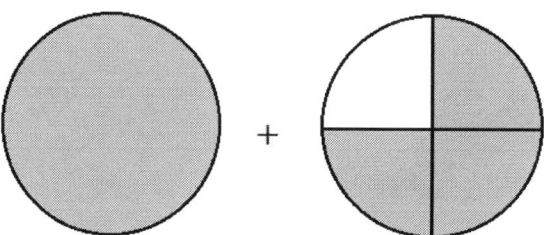

A. $1 + \frac{3}{4}$

B. $1 + \frac{1}{4}$

C. $4 + \frac{1}{2}$

D. $1 + \frac{4}{4}$

3) Mike rode his bike for 3 miles on Saturday and $\frac{3}{4}$ of a mile on Sunday. How many miles did Mike ride altogether?

A. $\frac{6}{4}$ B. $\frac{3}{2}$ C. $\frac{9}{4}$ D. $\frac{15}{4}$

4) Jessica added $\frac{5}{7}$ of a bag of soil to her garden. Her neighbor Charlie added 2 bags of soil to his garden. How much more soil did Charlie add than Jessica?

   A. $\frac{6}{7}$

   B. $\frac{19}{7}$

   C. $\frac{9}{7}$

   D. $\frac{10}{7}$

5) The fraction $\frac{28}{7}$ is equivalent to:

   A. 4
   B. 6
   C. 8
   D. 3

6) The result of $\frac{20}{10} + \frac{12}{4}$ is:

   A. $\frac{1}{4}$

   B. 4

   C. $\frac{32}{10}$

   D. 5

7) At Green Zoo, 20 of the animals are primates. Of the primates, $\frac{3}{4}$ are monkeys. What fraction of the animals at Green Zoo are monkeys?

   A. 12   B. 8   C. 16   D. 15

8) A school purchased 6 gallons of orange paint to decorate several of its classrooms. If each classroom needs $\frac{2}{3}$ of a gallon of paint, then how many classrooms will get painted?

   A. 15
   B. 9
   C. 10
   D. 7

9) A nursery is open two times a day: 2 hours in the morning and $\frac{15}{5}$ hours in the afternoon. How many hours is the nursery open every day?

   A. $\frac{17}{5}$ hours
   B. 4 hours
   C. 5 hours
   D. $\frac{12}{5}$ hours

10) Alice baked 36 cupcakes. Each cupcake is $\frac{2}{3}$ of a pound. If she puts 12 cupcakes in a box, what is the weight of each box?

    A. 8 pounds
    B. 12 pounds
    C. $\frac{25}{3}$ pounds
    D. $\frac{25}{3}$ pounds

11) Add $\frac{8}{13} + \frac{5}{13}$

    A. $\frac{14}{13}$
    B. 1
    C. $\frac{3}{13}$
    D. 2

12) Subtract $2 - \frac{3}{8}$

    A. $\frac{15}{8}$
    B. $\frac{13}{8}$
    C. $\frac{1}{8}$
    D. $\frac{5}{8}$

13) Multiply $10 \times \frac{1}{2}$

    A. 20
    B. 5
    C. $\frac{9}{2}$
    D. $\frac{20}{2}$

14) Divide $6 \div \frac{1}{6}$

    A. $\frac{1}{12}$
    B. 1
    C. $\frac{3}{6}$
    D. 36

15) An electrician has a piece of wire that is 12 feet long. He divides the wire into pieces that are $\frac{6}{7}$ feet long. How many pieces does he have?

A. 7   B. $\frac{18}{7}$ C. $\frac{82}{7}$ D. 14

Answer Key

1) C   2) A   3) D   4) C   5) A   6) D   7) D   8) B   9) C   10) A   11) B

12) B   13) B   14) D   15) D

Reflection on Learning

Answer the following reflection questions and feel free to discuss your responses with your teacher or a classmate.

1- What math idea, principle, or structure did you learn from this section?

2- What math concepts did you learn?

3- What procedures or method did you work on in this section?

4- What aspect of this section is still not 100% clear for you?

5- What else do you want your teacher to know?

CHAPTER 3

ALGEBRA

Key Vocabulary

> variable, multiplication, algebraic expression, equation, Cartesian coordinate plane, associative property, variables, number line

Ways of representing multiplication

We can use notational conventions and various ways of representing multiplication:

- Using a dot: $a \cdot b$ (*This represents the multiplication of variables a and b.*)

- Using parentheses: $(a)(b)$ (*This represents the multiplication of variables a and b.*)

- Using multiplication sign: $a \times b$ (*This represents the multiplication of variables a and b.*)

Example: Compute (4)(6)(5)

Step 1. Notice that we have a multiplication of three numbers.

Step 2. Multiply the three numbers.

$$(4)(6)(5) = \mathbf{120}$$

We can apply the **associative property** to solve this multiplication.

$$(4)(6)(5) = (24)(5) = 120$$

or

$$(4)(6)(5) = (4)(30) = 120$$

Notice that regrouping **does not change the result.**

Variables and algebraic expressions

A **variable** is a symbol for a number we don't know yet. It is usually a letter like **x** or **y**, but we can use any letter.

An **algebraic expression** is an expression involving numbers, parentheses, operation signs, and letters in which the letters can be replaced by numbers.

Examples of algebraic expressions:

$$2x + 5y, \quad 3a + b - 6, \quad 45d + 9t$$

Algebraic expressions are useful because they represent the value of an expression for all of the values a variable can take on. When we describe in words an expression that includes a variable, we are describing an algebraic expression—that is, an expression with a variable.

Example: Write an expression for "b increased by 15"

Step 1. Notice that the phrase "increased by" tells us to use addition.

Step 2. Thus, the expression is **b + 15**

Example: Write an expression for "a number divided by 8, and 6 is added to the result."

`**Step 1.** Let x be the number.

Step 2. Divide the number by 8

$$\frac{x}{8}$$

Step 3. Add 6 to the previous expression.

$$\frac{x}{8} + 6$$

Equations

An equation is a mathematical statement showing that two things are equal. For example, 9 + 10 is equal to 19.

$$9 + 10 = 19$$

In an equation, the left side is always equal to the right side. The most common equations contain one or more variables.

$$x - 15 = 34$$

To solve an equation, follow these steps:

Step 1. Figure out what to remove to find the value of the variable.

Step 2. To remove a number, add its opposite to both sides.

We can solve word problems **by using equations with a letter for the unknown number** to represent the problem or to represent simple contextual math situations.

Example: Last week Maurice had 287 dollars. Over the weekend, he earned money washing cars and now has 356 dollars. How much money did he make washing cars over the weekend?

Step 1. Let x be the money Maurice made washing cars.

Step 2. Set up the equation that represents the problem.

$$287 = 356 - x$$

Step 3. Now, begin to solve the equation. Remove x in the equation.

$$287 = 356 - \boxed{x}$$

Step 4. To remove $-x$, use its opposite. In this case, **add x** from **both sides** of the equation.

$$287 + x = 356 - x + x$$

Step 5. Subtract $x - x$:

$$287 + x = 356 - x + x$$

$$287 + x = 356$$

Step 6. We want to remove 287 in the equation. To remove 287, use its opposite. In this case, **subtract 287** from **both sides** of the equation.

$$287 - 287 + x = 356 - 287$$

Step 7. Subtract $287 - 287$ and $356 - 287$:

$$287 - 287 + x = 356 - 287$$

$$x = 69$$

Step 8. Thus, Maurice earned **$69** washing cars over the weekend.

Example: For a science project, 9 students each collected the same number of rocks. They collected 108 rocks in all. How many rocks did each student collect?

Step 1. Let r be the number of rocks that each student collected. Since each student collected r rocks, then 7 students collected $9 \cdot r$ (multiplication).

Step 2. Since the students collected 108 rocks in all, this value must be equal to $9 \cdot r$. Then we can set up an equation that represents the problem:

$$9 \cdot r = 108$$

Step 3. Now, we solve the equation. We want to remove 9 in the equation.

$$9 \cdot r = 108$$

Step 4. To remove 9, **divide everything by 9**. In this case, **divide both sides** of the equation by 9.

$$\frac{9 \cdot r}{9} = \frac{108}{9}$$

Step 5. Do the division.

$$\frac{9 \cdot r}{9} = \frac{108}{9}$$

$$\rightarrow r = 12$$

Step 6. Thus, each student collected **12 rocks**.

The coordinate system

The coordinate system is a two-dimensional **number line** formed by two perpendicular number lines called **axes**.

The horizontal axis is called the **x-axis** and the vertical axis is called the **y-axis.** The center of the coordinate system (where the lines intersect) is called the **origin**. The axes intersect when both x and y are zero. The coordinates of the origin are **(0, 0)**.

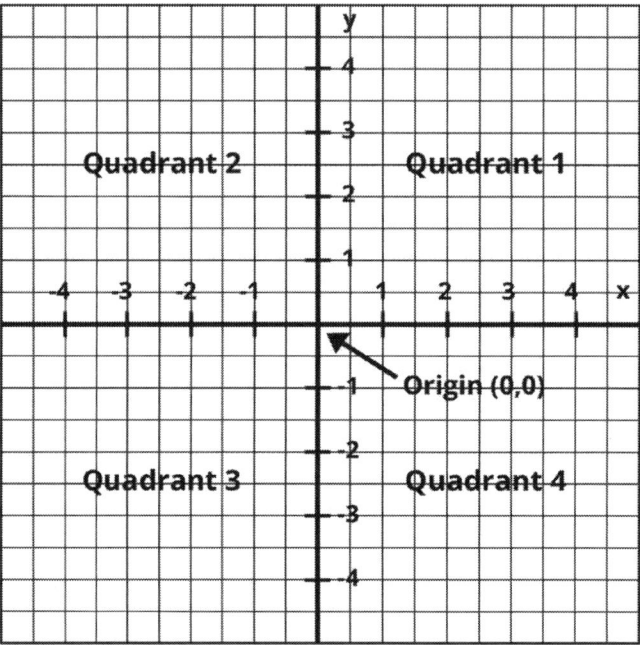

An **ordered pair** contains the coordinates of one point in the coordinate system. A **point** is named by its ordered pair in the form of (x, y). The first number always corresponds to the x-coordinate and the second to the y-coordinate.

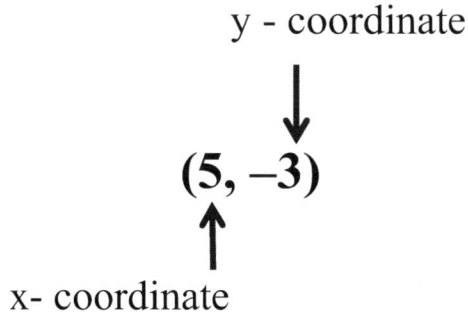

Example: What are the coordinates of point B?

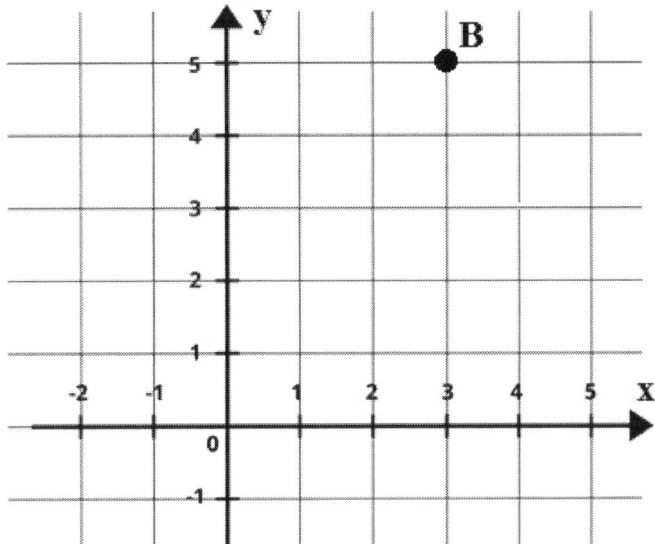

Step 1. Notice that the point B is found in Quadrant 1, so both its coordinates are positive.

Step 2. Note that the point B is 3 units of length from the x-axis and 5 units from the y-axis.

Step 3. Thus, the coordinates of point B are **(3, 5)**.

Example: What are the coordinates of point P?

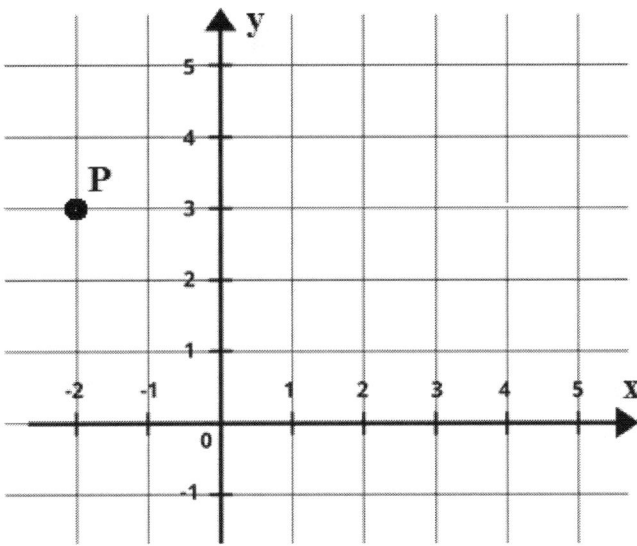

Step 1. Notice that point P is found in Quadrant 2, so the first coordinate is negative, and the second coordinate is positive.

Step 2. Note that the point P is a distance of 2 units of length from the x-axis and 3 units from the y-axis.

Step 3. Thus, the coordinates of point P are **(–2, 3)**.

Practice Exercises

1) Which of the following is a variable?

   A. 45
   B. 0.56
   C. y
   D. –15

2) Which of the following is an algebraic expression?

   A. 45 + 4
   B. 2 + 5 – 78
   C. 2a + 6b
   D. 6 + 1.2 = 7.2

3) Compute 3(12 + 5)

   A. 51
   B. 20
   C. 41
   D. 27

4) Which algebraic expression represents the phrase "23 less than the product of x and y"?

   A. 23x – y
   B. 23x·y
   C. x·y – 23
   D. 23 – x·y

5) Which algebraic expression represents this phrase "six times the sum of m and n"?

   A. m + n + 6
   B. 6(m + n)
   C. 6m + n
   D. n(6+m)

6) The sum of a number and 48 is equal to 173. What is the number?

   A. 95
   B. 125
   C. 221
   D. 143

7) Which equation represents the phrase "three times a number is equal to 321"?

   A. x + 3 = 321

   B. 3x = 321

   C. x + 321 = 3

   D. $\frac{x}{3} = 321$

8) Solve the equation 10y = 100

   A. y = 20
   B. y = 90
   C. y = 10
   D. y = 50

9) Melissa has several books in her house. She gives 17 books to her friends, and she keeps the remaining 21 books. Which equation can we use to find the total number of books (x) Melissa had in her house?

   A. x + 21 = 17
   B. x + 17 = 21
   C. 21 − x = 17
   D. x − 17 = 21

10) What are the coordinates of point M?

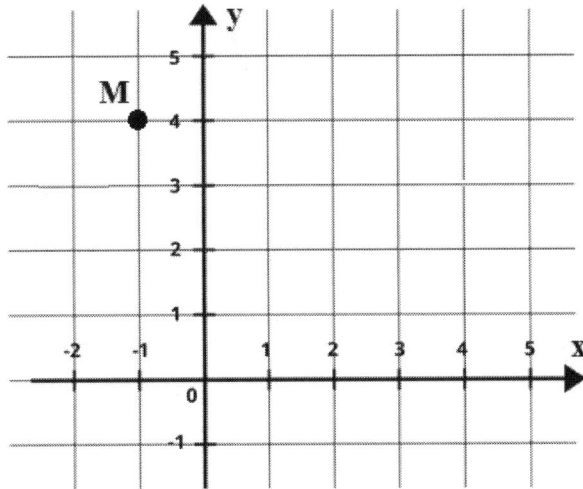

   A. (4, −1)
   B. (−1, 4)
   C. (4, 1)
   D. (−1, −4)

11) What are the coordinates of point C?

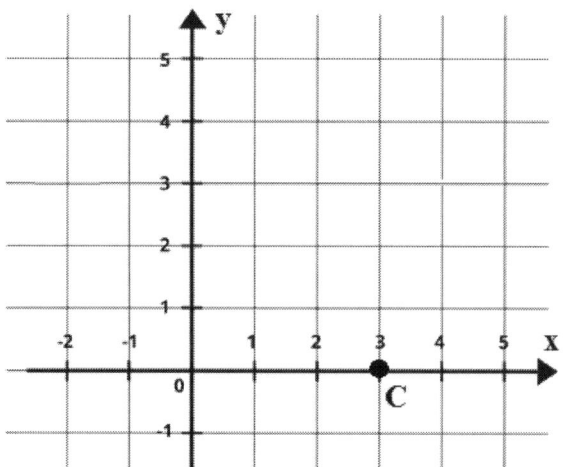

A. (0, 3)
B. (3, 3)
C. (3, 0)
D. (3, 1)

12) Solve the equation 7b = 77

A. b = 11
B. b = 70
C. b = 17
D. b = 10

13) Solve the equation 5x + 5 = 5

A. x = 1
B. x = 3
C. x = –1
D. x = 0

14) Compute (9 + 9)·(5 + 5)

A. 180
B. 95
C. 28
D. 170

15) Compute (1)(5)(7)

A. 13
B. 42
C. 35
D. 40

Answer Key

1) C   2) C   3) A   4) C   5) B   6) B   7) B   8) C   9) D   10) B   11) C

12) A   13) D   14) A   15) C

Reflection on Learning

Answer the following reflection questions and feel free to discuss your responses with your teacher or a classmate.

1- What math idea, principle, or structure did you learn from this section?

2- What math concepts did you learn?

3- What procedures or method did you work on in this section?

4- What aspect of this section is still not 100% clear for you?

5- What else do you want your teacher to know?

CHAPTER 4

GEOMETRY

Key Vocabulary

quadrilaterals, rectangle, square, parallelogram, three-dimensional shapes, figures, angles,

Quadrilaterals

Quadrilaterals are shapes that are formed by 4 sides. There are many types of quadrilaterals. A **rectangle** is a quadrilateral in which all angles are **right angles** (90°).

Rectangle

A **square** is a quadrilateral in which all sides **have equal length,** and all angles are **right angles** (90°).

Square

A **rhombus** is a quadrilateral in which all sides **have equal length.**

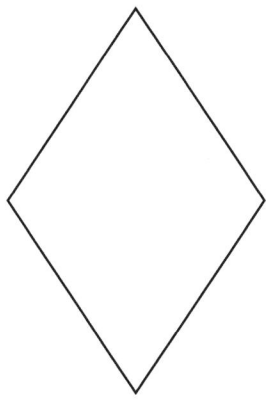

Rhombus

A parallelogram is a shape with 4 straight sides where **opposite sides are parallel**.

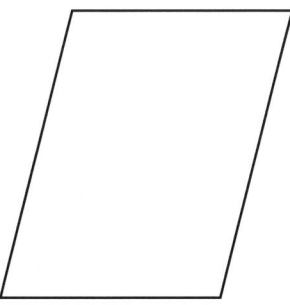

Parallelogram

Notice that squares, rectangles, and rhombuses are all **parallelograms**.

A **trapezoid** is a quadrilateral with exactly one pair of **parallel sides**.

Trapezoid

Three-dimensional shapes

There are two basic groups of three-dimensional shapes: prisms and pyramids.

A **prism** is a three-dimensional shape with two parallel faces called **bases**. The other faces are always **parallelograms**. The prism is named by the shape of its base.

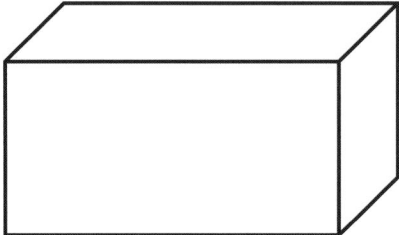

Rectangular prism

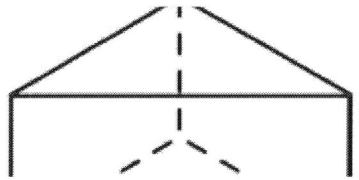

Triangular prism

A **cube** is a solid that has 6 identical square faces. Notice that a cube is still a prism.

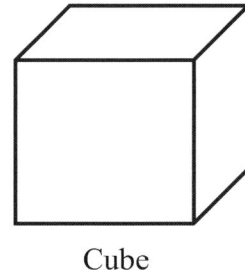

Cube

A **prism** is a three-dimensional shape whose base is a **polygon**. Each corner of a polygon is attached to a point called the **apex**. Each base edge and the apex form a **triangle**. There are many types of pyramids. They are named after the type of base they have.

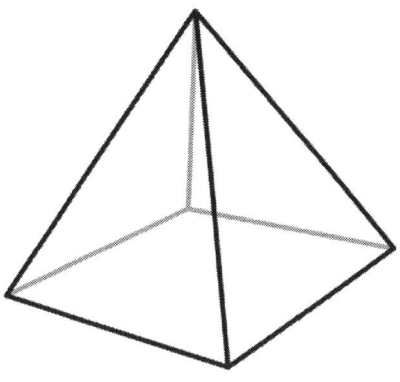

Square Pyramid

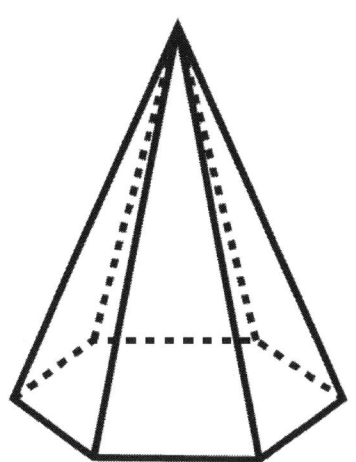

Hexagonal Pyramid

Several three-dimensional shapes can include at least some curves. In geometry, the most common curved solids are cylinders, cones, and spheres.

A **cylinder** is a closed solid that has two parallel (**usually circular**) bases connected by a curved surface.

A **cone** is a three-dimensional shape that has a circular base and a single **vertex** (the angular point of a polygon). If the vertex is over the center of the base, it is called a **right cone**. Otherwise, it is called an **oblique cone**.

A **sphere** is a geometrical figure that is perfectly round, three-dimensional and circular (like a ball). In other words, a sphere is the set of all points equidistant from a single point in space called the **center**.

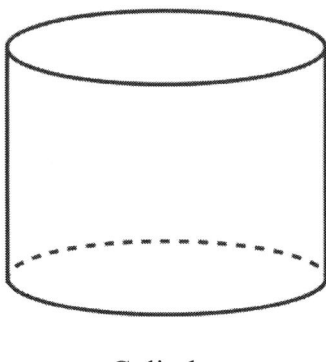

Cylinder

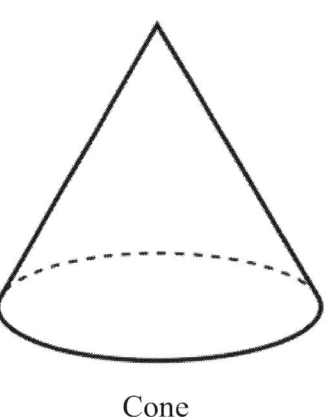

Cone

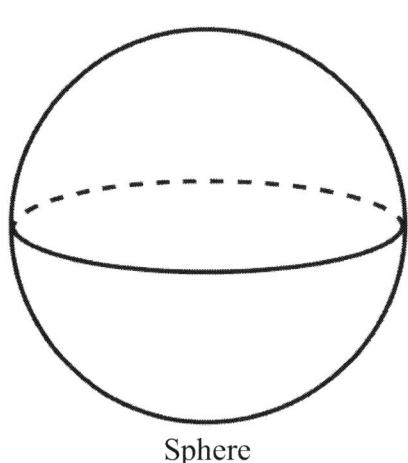

Sphere

Three-dimensional shapes using nets

A **net** is a two-dimensional drawing of a three-dimensional shape. We can represent a three-dimensional shape as a net composed of rectangles, triangles, and circles.

Example: Which figure will this net make?

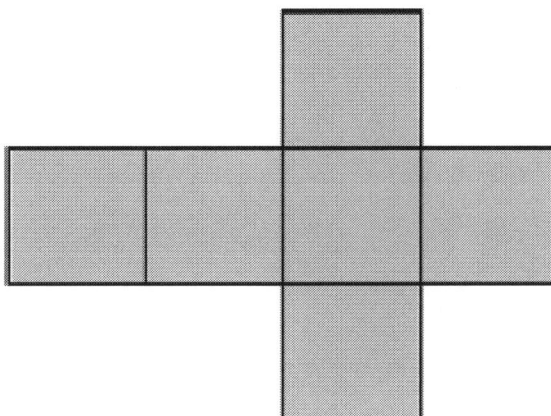

Step 1. Note that the net is formed by six **squares.**

Step 2. The net can be folded to form a **cube.**

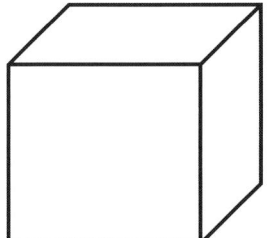

Practice Exercises

1) Which shape is **not** a parallelogram?

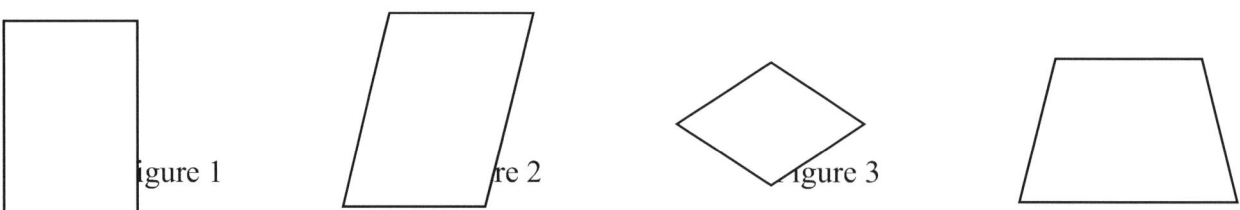

A. Figure 4
B. Figure 3
C. Figure 1
D. Figure 2

2) How many right angles does a rectangle have?

A. 2
B. 4
C. 5
D. None

3) What are the shapes that are formed by four sides called?

A. Pyramids
B. Cubes
C. Quadrilaterals
D. Prims

4) What is the quadrilateral with exactly one pair of parallel sides called?

A. Square
B. Rhombus
C. Rectangle
D. Trapezoid

5) How many corners does a rhombus have?

   A. 3
   B. 5
   C. 4
   D. 2

6) Which of the following is a prism?

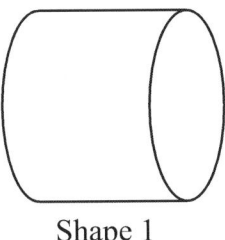
Shape 1

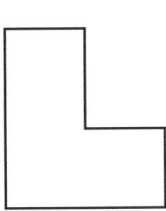
Shape 2

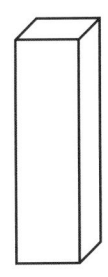
Shape 3

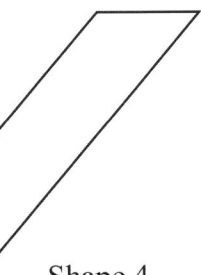
Shape 4

   A. Shape 4
   B. Shape 1
   C. Shape 2
   D. Shape 3

7) What is the name of the following three-dimensional shape?

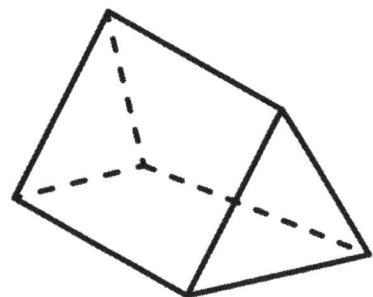

   A. Rectangular pyramid
   B. Triangular prism
   C. Rectangular prism
   D. Triangular pyramid

8) How many faces does a cube have?

A. 4
B. 6
C. 8
D. 10

9) What is the three-dimensional shape that has a circular base and a single vertex called?

A. Pyramid
B. Prism
C. Cylinder
D. Cone

10) Which shape is a cylinder?

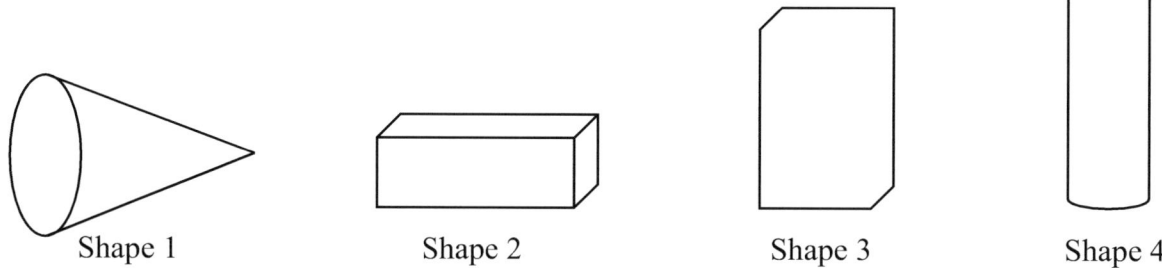

A. Shape 3
B. Shape 1
C. Shape 4
D. Shape 2

11) How many triangular faces does a square pyramid have?

A. 3
B. 4
C. 5
D. None

12) What figure will this net make?

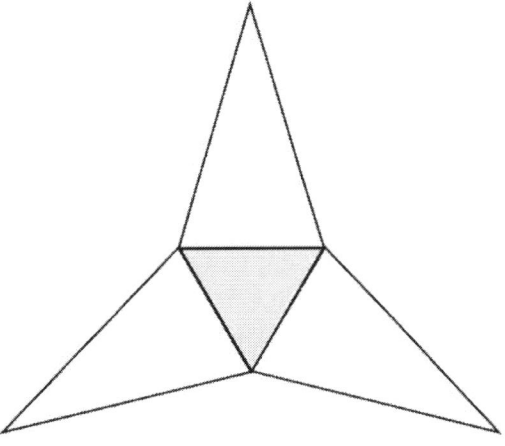

   A. Triangular prism
   B. Triangular pyramid
   C. Cube
   D. Rectangular pyramid

13) What figure will this net make?

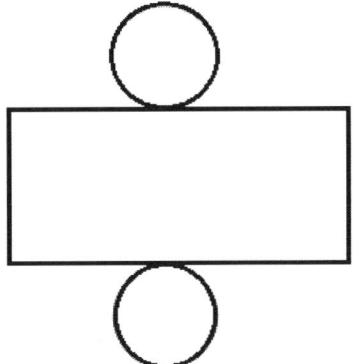

   A. Cone
   B. Rectangular prism
   C. Cylinder
   D. Sphere

14) What figure will this net make?

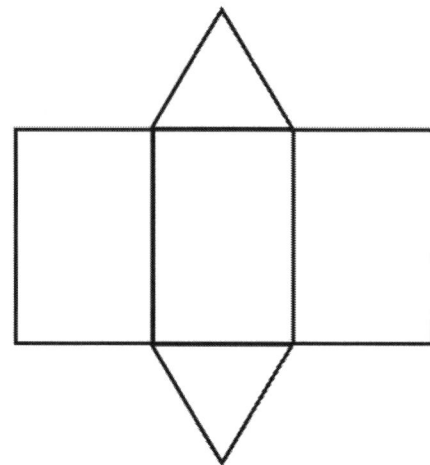

   A. Triangular Prism
   B. Triangular Pyramid
   C. Cube
   D. Rectangular Prism

15) The following solid is formed by identical cubes. How many cubes are in the solid?

A. 19
B. 21
C. 27
D. 30

Answer Key

1) A   2) B   3) C   4) D   5) C   6) D   7) B   8) B   9) D   10) C   11) B

12) B   13) C   14) A   15) C

Reflection on learning

Answer the following reflection questions and feel free to discuss your responses with your teacher or a classmate.

1- What math idea, principle, or structure did you learn from this section?

2- What math concepts did you learn?

3- What procedures or method did you work on in this section?

4- What aspect of this section is still not 100% clear for you?

5- What else do you want your teacher to know?

CHAPTER 5

MEASUREMENT AND DATA

Key Vocabulary

> temperature, scale, customary units, linear measurement, units of weight, units of capacity, area, length, volume, gallon, cup

Measuring temperature

Temperature is involved in many aspects of our daily lives. Temperature can be negative or positive. The higher the **positive** temperature, the hotter it is. The lower the **negative** temperature, the colder it is. Temperature is measured in degrees Celsius (°C) or degrees Fahrenheit (°F)

Example: What is the temperature shown on the thermometer?

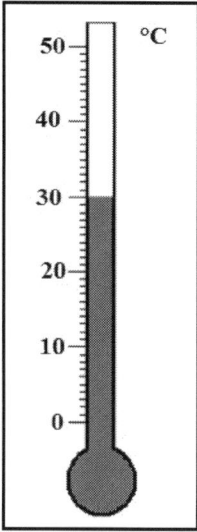

Step 1. Notice that the thermometer indicates 30. This value is above 0° C. This means that the temperature is positive.

Step 2. The temperature is **30°C** or **+30°C**.

Example: What is the temperature shown on the thermometer?

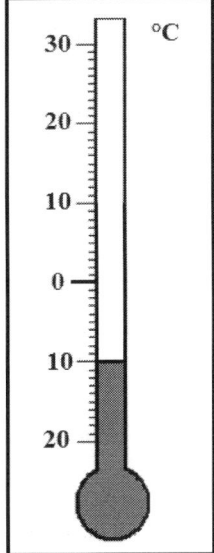

Step 1. Notice that the thermometer indicates 10. This value is below 0° C. This means that the temperature is negative.

Step 2. The temperature is **−10°C**.

Measurement of time

To measure the time, we use **hours** and **minutes**. For example, if the time is **6:13**, the hour is **6** and the minutes are **13**. Another way to say this is that the time is 13 minutes after 6 o'clock.

To visualize the time, we use **analog clocks**. There are two hands on an analog clock. The short hand is the **hour hand**. The long hand is the **minute hand.**

Analog Clock

We use the short hand to read the hour. The hour is the number the short hand is either pointing to or has recently passed.

We use the long hand to read the minutes. Take the number that the short hand is pointing to and **multiply it by 5** to get the minutes. When it is pointing to the number 12, it is the top of the hour.

Example: What time is it?

Step 1. Notice that the hour hand is between 3 and 4, so it is after 3 o'clock but not yet 4 o'clock. Thus, the hour is 3.

Step 2. Notice that the minute hand is pointing to the number 8. This means that it is **8 x 5 = 40 minutes** past the hour.

Step 3. Thus, the time is **3:40**.

We can also visualize the time using **digital clocks**. Digital clocks show the time using only numbers.

Metric units and customary U.S. units of linear measurement

We can measure how long or tall things are, or the distance between things, such as cities. These are all examples of length measurements. Length is typically measured in **metric units** or **customary units**.

Centimeters and **meters** are examples of metric units. **Inches** and **feet** are examples of customary units. To measure lengths, we can use some tools (rulers and yardsticks).

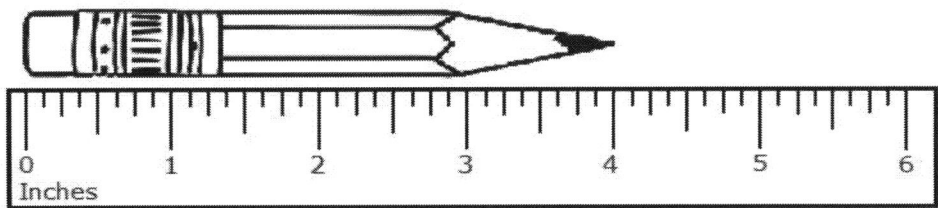

The length of the pencil is 4 inches.

Small metric units of length are called **millimeters.** The symbol for millimeter is **mm.** When we have something that is 10 millimeters long, it is said to be 1 **centimeter**. The symbol for centimeter is **cm.** In other words,

1 centimeter = 10 millimeters
1 cm = 10 mm

A **meter** is longer than a **centimeter.** There are 100 centimeters in 1 meter.

1 meter = 100 centimeters

In other words,

1 meter = 100 centimeters = 1,000 millimeters
1 m = 100 cm = 1,000 mm

Small customary units of length are called **inches.** When we have 12 inches together, it is known as a **foot**.

1 foot = 12 inches

Compared to metric units, a meter is a **little longer than** 3 feet. Compared to metric units, a centimeter is **shorter than** an inch.

When 3 feet are together, this is called a **yard**.

1 yard = 3 feet

When we put together 1.760 yards, we have a **mile**.

1 mile = 1.760 yards.

When we need to measure greater distances, such as how far we are going to drive or fly, the distance between cities, we measure that distance using **miles** or **kilometers**.

1 km = 1,000 m
1 mile = 1.609 kilometers

We can calculate with and convert between metric units of linear measurement.

Example: Convert 13 kilometers into meters.

    Step 1. Identify the larger unit and the smaller unit.

        The larger unit is the kilometer and the smaller unit is the meter.

    Step 2. Since we are going from a larger unit to a smaller unit, we must **multiply.**

    Step 3. Multiply to find the number of meters in 13 kilometers.

$$13 \times 1000 \text{ m} = \mathbf{13{,}000 \text{ m}} \quad \text{(Recall: 1 km = 1000 m)}$$

Example: Convert 76 centimeters to meters.

    Step 1. Identify the larger unit and the smaller unit.

        The larger unit is the meter and the smaller unit is the centimeter.

    Step 2. Since we are going from a smaller unit to a larger unit, we must **divide.**

    Step 3. Divide to find the number of meters in 76 centimeters.

$$76 \div 100 \text{ m} = \mathbf{0.76 \text{ m}} \quad \text{(Recall: 1 m = 100 cm)}$$

We can calculate with and convert between customary units of linear measurement.

Example: Convert 96 inches to feet.

    Step 1. Identify the larger unit and the smaller unit.

        The larger unit is the foot and the smaller unit is the inch.

    Step 2. Since we are going from a smaller unit to a larger unit, we must **divide.**

    Step 3. Divide to find the number of feet in 96 inches.

$$96 \div 12 \text{ feet} = \mathbf{8 \text{ feet}} \quad \text{(Recall: 1 foot = 12 inches)}$$

Example: Convert 54 yards into feet.

Step 1. Identify the larger unit and the smaller unit.

The larger unit is the yard and the smaller unit is the foot.

Step 2. Since we are going from a larger unit to a smaller unit, we must **multiply**.

Step 3. Multiply to find the number of feet in 54 yards:

54 x 3 feet = **162 feet**   (Recall: 1 yard = 3 feet)

Remember:

> 1 foot = 12 inches
>
> 1 yard = 3 feet = 36 inches
>
> 1 mile = 1,760 yards = 5,280 feet = 63,360 inches

We can compare the measurement of one object to another using metric units or customary units of linear measurement.

Example: The glass is about 7 inches tall. About how tall is the pitcher?

Step 1. We know that the **height of the glass is 7 inches.** Notice that the height of the pitcher is about **twice** of the height of the glass.

Step 2. Thus, the height of the pitcher is about **14 inches**.

Customary U.S. units of weight

The smallest unit of mass is **ounces (oz)**. A slice of pizza is about one ounce. If we have 16 ounces, it can also be called a **pound (lb)**. Typically, a pound is the unit we use to measure the weight of people.

$$1 \text{ pound} = 16 \text{ ounces}$$

When we put together 2000 pounds, we have a **ton**. In other words,

$$1 \text{ pound} = 16 \text{ ounces}$$

$$1 \text{ ton} = 2{,}000 \text{ pounds} = 32{,}000 \text{ ounces}$$

We can calculate with and convert between customary units of weight.

Example: Convert 43 pounds to ounces.

    Step 1. Identify the larger unit and the smaller unit.

        The larger unit is the pound and the smaller unit is the ounce.

    Step 2. Since we are going from a larger unit to a smaller unit, we must **multiply.**

    Step 3. Multiply to find the number of ounce in 43 pounds:

$$43 \times 16 \text{ ounces} = \mathbf{688 \text{ ounces}} \quad (\text{Recall: } 1 \text{ pound} = 16 \text{ ounces})$$

Customary U.S. units of capacity

The U.S. customary capacity or volume measurement units are ounces, cups, pints, quarts, and gallons.

The smallest unit of capacity is **ounces** (or **fluid ounces**). A **cup** is equal to 8 ounces.

$$1 \text{ cup} = 8 \text{ fluid ounces}$$

When we put together 2 cups, we have a **pint**.

$$1 \text{ pint} = 2 \text{ cups}$$

A **quart (qt)** is the same thing as 4 cups or 2 pints.

$$1 \text{ quart} = 2 \text{ pints} = 4 \text{ cups}$$

The largest unit of capacity is **gallon (gal)**. A gallon is the same as 16 cups or 8 pints or 4 quarts.

1 gallon = 4 quarts = 8 pints = 16 cups

We can calculate with and convert between customary units of capacity.

Example: Convert 592 cups to gallons.

   Step 1. Identify the larger unit and the smaller unit.

   The larger unit is the gallon and the smaller unit is the cup.

   Step 2. Since we are going from a smaller unit to a larger unit, we must **divide.**

   Step 3. Divide to find the number of feet in 592 cups:

   $592 \div 16$ feet = **37 gallons**   (Recall: 1 gallon = 16 cups)

Area of common figures

Area is the amount of two-dimensional space inside a closed two-dimensional figure. A square with side lengths 1 unit, called **a unit square**, is said to have "one square unit" of area, and can be used to measure area.

A **square inch** is a unit of area equal to the area of a square with sides of one inch.

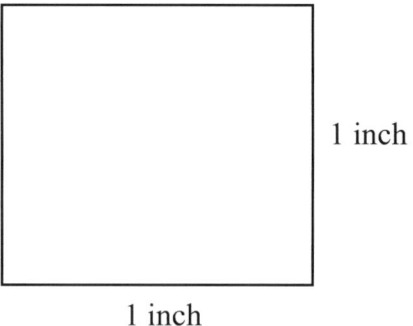

Area of square = 1in²

To find the area of a rectangle, we multiply the length by the width.

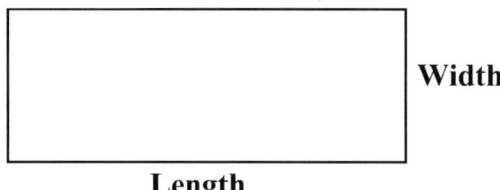

Area of rectangle = Length x Width

Example: Find the area of the following rectangle.

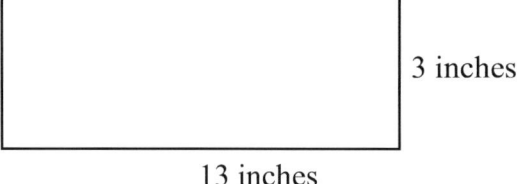

Step 1. Note that the width of the rectangle is 3 inches and the length is 13 inches.

Step 2. Multiply the length by the width.

$$13 \text{ inches} \times 3 \text{ inches} = 39 \text{ in}^2$$

Step 3. Thus, the area of the rectangle is **39 in²**

Practice Exercises

1) What is the temperature shown on the thermometer?

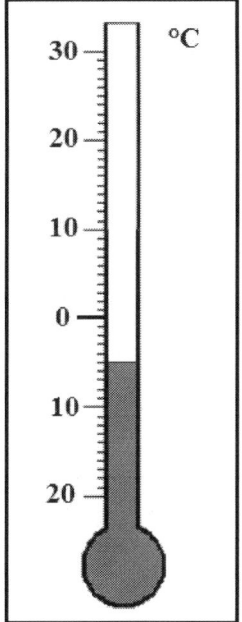

A. 15°C
B. −15°C
C. −5°C
D. 5°C

2) What time is it?

A. 2 hours and 11 minutes
B. 1 hour and 55 minutes
C. 2 hours and 55 minutes
D. 11 hours and 2 minutes

3) Which of the following is larger?

A. 10 meters
B. 100 centimeters
C. 2 kilometers
D. 500 millimeters

4) Frank rode 3 miles on his bike. Mr. Brown rode 3,520 yards on his bike, and Melissa rode 5,280 feet on her bike. Who rode the farthest?

A. Melissa
B. Mr. Brown
C. Frank
D. There is not enough information given.

5) Emily measured a line for her art project. The line is 48 inches long. How many feet long is the line?

A. 6
B. 5
C. 2
D. 4

6) Teddy weighs 95 pounds. What is Teddy's weight in ounces?

A. 3,040 oz.
B. 1,520 oz.
C. 1,200 oz.
D. 190 oz.

7) The glass is about 9 inches tall. About how tall is the chair?

A. 62 inches B. 49 inches
C. 26 inches D. 36 inches

8) Which of the following is smaller?

A. 2 gallons
B. 12 quarts
C. 128 ounces
D. 48 pints

9) Convert 10 kilometers to meters.

A. 10,000 meters
B. 1,000 meters
C. 100 meters
D. 0,01 meters

10) Convert 1,296 inches to yards.

A. 12 yards
B. 24 yards
C. 36 yards
D. 42 yards

11) Convert 5 tons to ounces.

A. 16,000 ounces
B. 10,000 pounds
C. 1,600,000 ounces
D. 1,000 pounds

12) What is the missing number?

800 cups = _____ gallons.

A. 500
B. 25
C. 250
D. 50

13) What is the missing number?

_____ miles = 126,720 inches.

A. 1
B. 3
C. 5
D. 2

14) What is the area of the following rectangle?

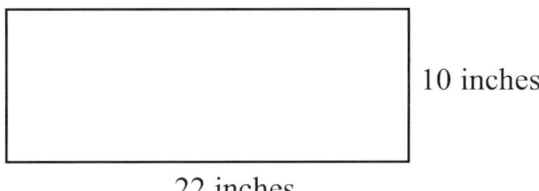

A. 220 inches
B. 32 square inches
C. 220 square inches
D. 202 inches

15) What is the area of the following rectangle?

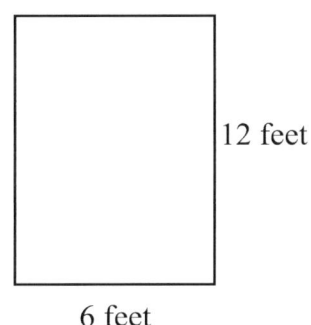

A. 72 square feet
B. 62 square feet
C. 72 square inches
D. 38 square feet

Answer Key

1) C 2) B 3) C 4) C 5) D 6) B 7) D 8) C 9) A 10) C 11) B

12) D 13) D 14) C 15) A

Reflection on Learning

Answer the following reflection questions and feel free to discuss your responses with your teacher or a classmate.

1- What math idea, principle, or structure did you learn from this section?

2- What math concepts did you learn?

3- What procedures or method did you work on in this section?

4- What aspect of this section is still not 100% clear for you?

5- What else do you want your teacher to know?

CHAPTER 6

DATA ANALYSIS

Key Vocabulary

data set, list, table, chart, sample, average, distribution of the data, spread of the data, median, mode, center,

Center, spread, and overall shape

When we talk about center, shape, or spread, we are talking about the **distribution** of data, or how data is spread across a graph or chart.

The center of a distribution is a measurement of what a **typical value** would be. We have two measurements for the center of a distribution, the **mean** and the **median.**

The **spread in data** is the measure of how far the numbers in a data set are away from the mean or median. The simplest way to find the spread in a data set is to identify the **range**, which is the difference between the highest and lowest values in a data set.

The number that appears the most often in a data set is called **mode**.

The **shape of a distribution** is described by the number of its peaks and how symmetrical it is, its tendency to skew, or its uniformity.

Shapes of Distributions

Symmetric

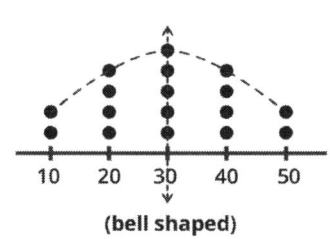
(bell shaped)

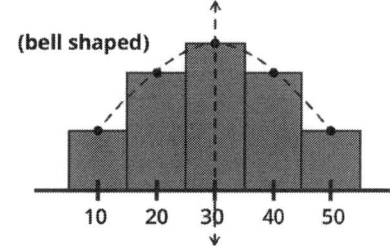
(bell shaped)

Skewed

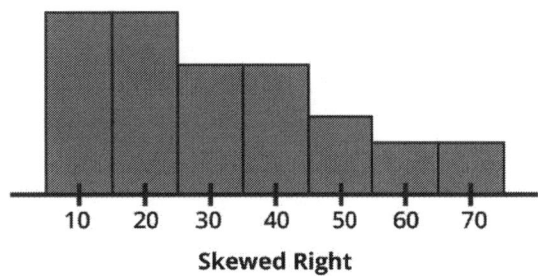
Skewed Right

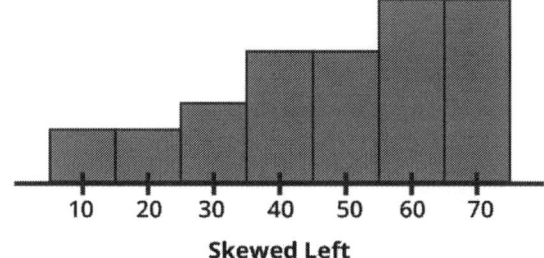
Skewed Left

Uniform

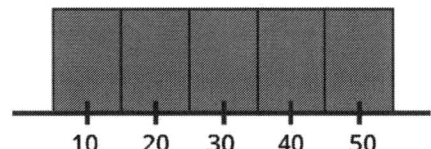

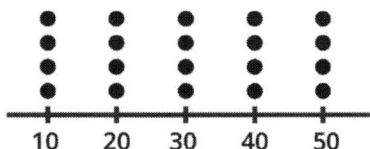

The mean is the **average** of the numbers. To calculate the mean, add all the values, then divide by the total number of values.

Example: Calculate the mean from the following data set:

$$30, 15, 25, 34, 40, 52, 18, 36,$$

Step 1. Add all the numbers.

$$30 + 15 + 25 + 34 + 40 + 52 + 18 + 36 = 250$$

Step 2. There are 8 values in the data set, so divide 250 by 8

$$250 \div 8 = 31.25$$

Step 3. Thus, the mean for the data set is **31.25**

Example: Calculate the median and the range of the following data set:

10, 7, 3, 1, 12, 5

Step 1. The median is the **middle** of a sorted list of numbers. To calculate the median, first place all of the values in numerical order.

1, 3, 5, 7, 10, 12

If we have an odd number of values, the median is the middle number. However, if we have an even number of values, the median will be the **mean** of the two values in the center of the data set.

Step 2. We have an even number of values, so calculate the mean of the two central values.

1, 3, (5, 7), 10, 12

$$\text{Mean} = \frac{5+7}{2} = \frac{12}{2} = 6$$

Step 3. Thus, the median for the data set is 6.

Step 4. To calculate the range of the data set, subtract the highest value from the lowest value.

Range = 14 − 6 = **8**

Practice Exercises

1) The measurement for the center of a distribution is the:

A. Range
B. Mode
C. Median
D. Data set

2) What is the shape of the distribution shown here?

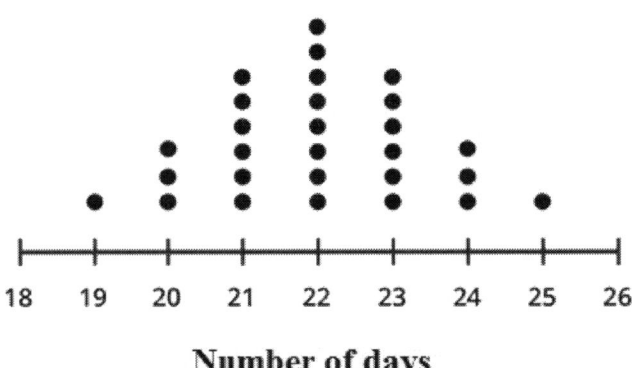

Number of days

   A. Uniform
   B. Symmetric
   C. Skewed
   D. None of the above

3) What is the shape of the distribution shown here?

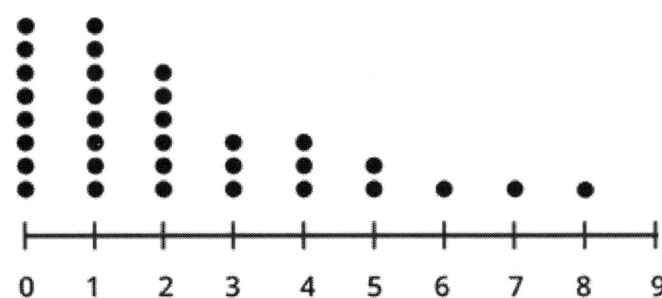

   A. Skewed
   B. Uniform
   C. Symmetric
   D. None of the above

4) The difference between the highest and lowest values in a data set is the:

   A) Average
   B) Mode
   C) Range
   D) Mean

5) The middle of a sorted list of numbers is the:

   A. Mean
   B. Median
   C. Range
   D. Mode

Look at the following bar chart.

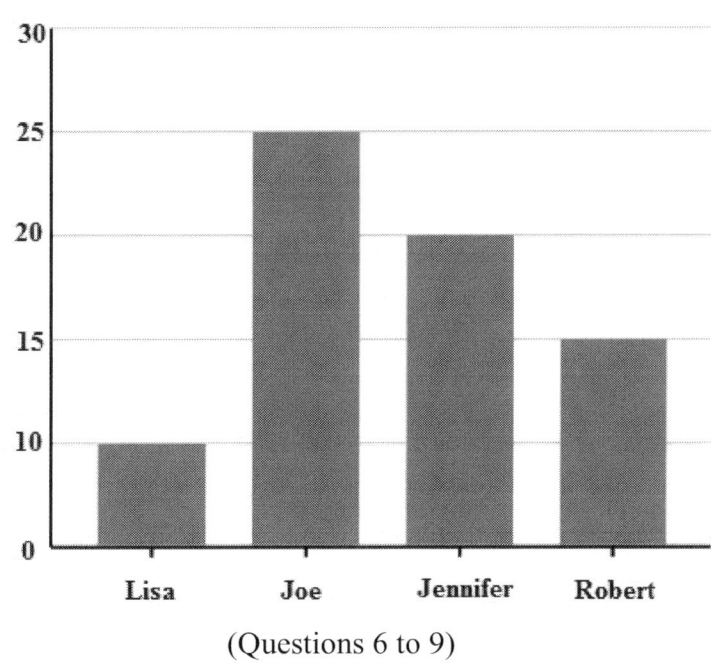

(Questions 6 to 9)

6) What is the lowest value in the data set?

   A. 0
   B. 10
   C. 15
   D. 25

7) What is the highest value in the data set?

   A. 30
   B. 20
   C. 25
   D. 15

8) What is the mean of the data set?

   A. 20
   B. 15.5
   C. 18
   D. 17.5

9) What is the range of the data set?

   A. 15
   B. 25
   C. 30
   D. 10

Look at the following data set.

$$9, 1, 10, 25, 10, 12, 1, 8, 2, 10$$

(Questions 10 to 13)

10) What is the mean of the data set?

   A. 10
   B. 9
   C. 8.8
   D. 11.5

11) What is the median of the data set?

   A. 9.5
   B. 9
   C. 10
   D. 10.5

12) What is the range of the data set?

   A. 25
   B. 24
   C. 1
   D. 10

13) What is the mode of the data set?

   A. 2
   B. 25
   C. 10
   D. 1

14) The mean of 15, 24, and B is 20. What is B?

   A. 22
   B. 21
   C. 26
   D. 19

15) The number that appears the most often is the:

   A. Average
   B. Median
   C. Range
   D. Mode

Answer Key

1) C   2) B   3) A   4) C   5) B   6) B   7) C   8) D   9) A   10) C   11) A

12) B   13) C   14) B   15) D

Reflection on Learning

Answer the following reflection questions and feel free to discuss your responses with your teacher or a classmate.

1- What math idea, principle, or structure did you learn from this section?

2- What math concepts did you learn?

3- What procedures or method did you work on in this section?

4- What aspect of this section is still not 100% clear for you?

5- What else do you want your teacher to know?

CHAPTER 7

PRACTICE TESTS

The real CASAS Math GOALS test has 40 items and is 60 minute long. So, to practice effectively learners should complete each practice test (40 test items) in 60 minutes. In other words, they will have 1 minute 30 seconds per math question. Learners may be allowed to use a basic calculator during test.

Go to the next page to start practice test # 1.

MATH PRACTICE TEST # 1

40 Questions in 60 minutes

1. Which is another way to show 1,539?

   A. 1,500 x 39
   B. 1,500 + 30 + 19
   C. 1,000 + 500 + 30 + 9
   D. 1,000 + 300 + 50 + 9

2. A food market bought 2,405 boxes of cookies last year. They bought 1,848 boxes of cookies this year. How many boxes of cookies did the food market buy altogether?

   A. 4,503
   B. 5,321
   C. 3,523
   D. 4,523

3. The number 15 can be written as:

   A. $\frac{30}{3}$

   B. $\frac{30}{2}$

   C. $\frac{15}{3}$

   D. $\frac{45}{5}$

4. The result of $6 \div \frac{3}{4}$ is:

   A. $\frac{18}{4}$

   B. 5

   C. $\frac{9}{4}$

   D. 8

5. Of the students in Henry's class, 15 students have a pet dog. Of the students who have a dog, $\frac{3}{5}$ also have a cat. How many students in Henry's class have both a cat and a dog?

   A. 9
   B. 12
   C. 5
   D. 8

6. Which of the following is an algebraic expression?

   A. 56 + 0.45
   B. 2x + 3y − 5
   C. −4
   D. 100 − 40 = 60

7. The sum of a number and 123 is equal to 500. What is the number?

   A. 257
   B. 623
   C. 377
   D. 367

8. Which equation represents the phrase "a number divided by 7 is equal to 186"?

   A. 7x = 186

   B. $\frac{7}{x} = 186$

   C. $\frac{186}{x} = 7$

   D. $\frac{x}{7} = 186$

9. Which shape is a parallelogram?

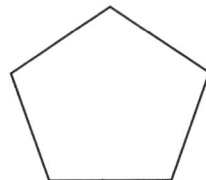 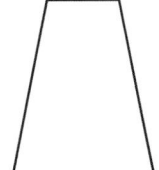 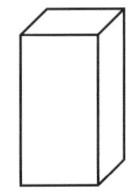 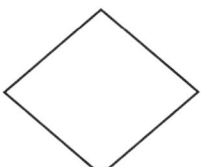

　　Figure 1　　　　　Figure 2　　　　　Figure 3　　　　　Figure 4

A. Figure 2
B. Figure 3
C. Figure 4
D. Figure 1

10. How many sides does a rhombus have?

A. 4
B. 2
C. 5
D. None the above

11. What figure will this net make?

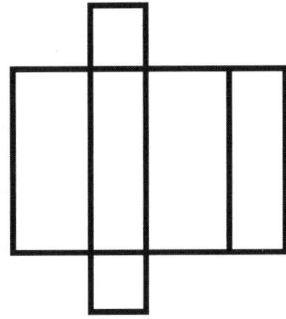

A. Rectangular pyramid
B. Cube
C. Cylinder
D. Rectangular prism

12. What is the temperature shown on the thermometer?

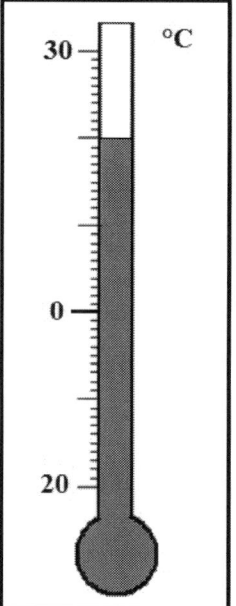

   A. 15°C
   B. 20°C
   C. −15°C
   D. −20°C

13. What time is it?

   A. 12:06
   B. 12:30
   C. 6:00
   D. 6:12

14. Which of the following is smaller?

   A. 17,600 yards
   B. 5 miles
   C. 36,960 feet
   D. 380,160 inches

15. What is the mean of this data set?

    5, 12, 18, 40, 50

    A. 25
    B. 28
    C. 30
    D. 50

16. What is the median of this data set?

    17, 19, 8, 1, 5, 29, 48, 33, 21

    A. 5
    B. 29
    C. 48
    D. 19

17. Which of the following is an odd number?

    A. 507
    B. 218
    C. 930
    D. 772

18. A construction company bought 1.09 tons of gravel and 0.84 tons of sand. How many tons of material did the company buy in all?

    A. 1.83
    B. 2.07
    C. 1.93
    D. 1.94

19. If 2,835 pounds of rice is packed in 63 bags, how much rice will each bag contain?

    A. 38 pounds
    B. 45 pounds
    C. 42 pounds
    D. 51 pounds

20. Which of the following is an even number?

    A. 987
    B. 515
    C. 109
    D. 302

21. Which of the following sums represents the following figure?

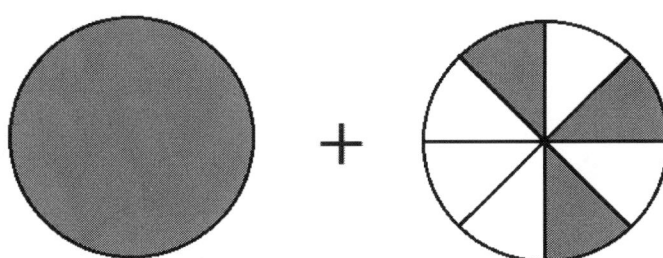

A. $1 + \frac{3}{8}$

B. $1 + \frac{5}{4}$

C. $\frac{1}{8} + \frac{3}{8}$

D. $1 + \frac{1}{8}$

22. The fraction $\frac{60}{4}$ is equivalent to:

   A. 12
   B. 20
   C. 15
   D. 16

23. Michael rode the bus 2 miles, then walked $\frac{2}{3}$ of a mile to get home. How much farther did Michael ride than walk?

   A. $\frac{8}{3}$ miles

   B. $\frac{4}{3}$ miles

   C. $\frac{1}{3}$ mile

   D. $\frac{5}{3}$ miles

24. The solution of the equation 12y = 84 is:

   A. y = 72
   B. y = 9
   C. y = 28
   D. y = 7

25. Which point has the coordinates (– 4, 2)?

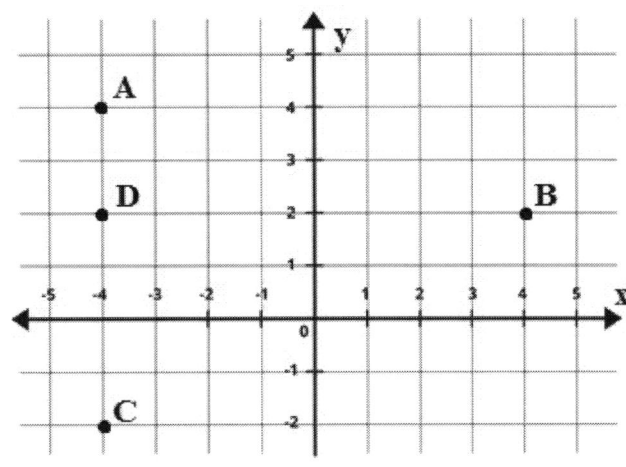

   A. Point B
   B. Point D
   C. Point C
   D. Point A

26. The result of (8 + 10)·(1 + 3) is:

   A. 22
   B. 57
   C. 72
   D. 84

27. Which shape is a cone?

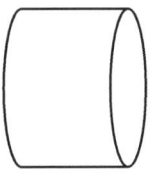 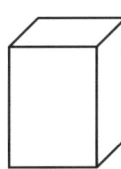 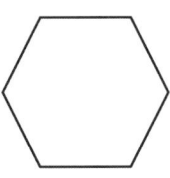 

Shape 1   Shape 2   Shape 3   Shape 4

   A. Shape 4
   B. Shape 1
   C. Shape 3
   D. Shape 2

28. What is the name of the following three-dimensional shape?

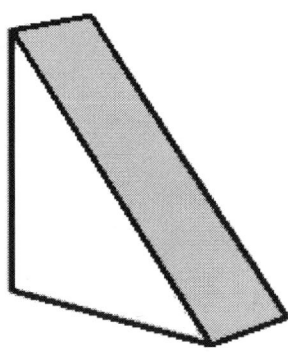

   A. Rectangular pyramid
   B. Rectangular prism
   C. Triangular pyramid
   D. Triangular prism

29. The three-dimensional shape that has two parallel circular bases connected by a curved surface is:

   A. A cone
   B. A cylinder
   C. A sphere
   D. A cube

30. What is the missing number?

   13 gallons = ____ pints

   A. 52
   B. 104
   C. 1,664
   D. 93

31. Pamela weighs 1,760 ounces. What is Pamela's weight in pounds?

   A. 110 pounds
   B. 100 pounds
   C. 55 pounds
   D. 123 pounds

32. What is the temperature shown on the thermometer?

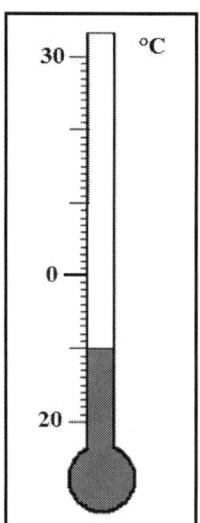

   A. 5°C
   B. −5°C
   C. 10°C
   D. −10°C

33. What is the mode of this data set?

37, 65, 29, 100, 37, 41, 9, 37, 100, 66, 37, 25, 8, 37, 73, 100

A. 100
B. 9
C. 37
D. 73

34. What is the shape of the distribution shown here?

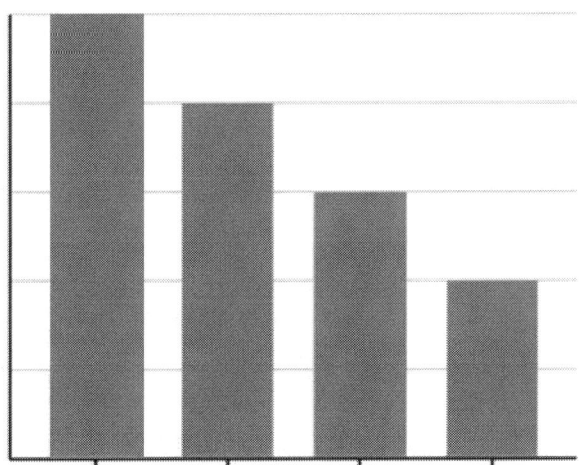

A. Uniform
B. Skewed right
C. Symmetric
D. Skewed left

35. The result of $3 + \frac{3}{7}$ is:

A. $\frac{24}{7}$

B. $\frac{31}{7}$

C. $\frac{13}{7}$

D. $\frac{21}{3}$

36. The result of 14.65 x 2.6 is:

A. 28.07
B. 29.094
C. 38.09
D. 41.093

37. The number 36 can be written as:

    A. $\dfrac{108}{4}$

    B. $\dfrac{72}{3}$

    C. $\dfrac{360}{5}$

    D. $\dfrac{36}{1}$

38. Which algebraic expression represents the phrase "nine times the difference between x and y"?

    A. 9x – y
    B. 9 + x – y
    C. 9(x – y)
    D. 9(x + y)

39. What is the area of the following rectangle?

    4.7 inches
    16. 5 inches

    A. 77.55 square inches
    B. 7.755 square inches
    C. 89.56 square inches
    D. 70.85 square inches

40. What is the missing number?

    1.5 yards = _____ inches

    A. 36
    B. 42
    C. 48
    D. 54

Reflection on Practice Test # 1

Answer the following reflection questions and feel free to discuss your responses with your teacher or a classmate.

1- How do you feel about your performance on the practice test?

2- Was anything too hard for you? What was it?

3- Was anything too easy for you? What was it?

4- What math procedures do you still need to review?

5- List the math procedures and skills that you need to work on or to practice more.

6- What else do you want your teacher to know?

MATH PRACTICE TEST # 2

40 Questions in 60 minutes

1. How do you write 0.07 in words?

    A. Seven tenths
    B. Seven hundredths
    C. Seventy
    D. Seventeen

2. A 4-digit number has 3 in the thousands place, 8 in the tens place, and 0s elsewhere. What is the number?

    A. 3,008
    B. 3,800
    C. 8,030
    D. 3,080

3. What is another way to show 803?

    A. 800 + 3
    B. 80 + 100 + 3
    C. 100 + 30 + 8
    D. 8(100 + 3)

4. The number 20 can be written as:

    A. $\frac{40}{4}$

    B. 10 + 2

    C. $\frac{80}{6}$

    D. $\frac{40}{2}$

5. The result of $10 \div \frac{1}{10}$ is:

    A. 100

    B. $\frac{1}{100}$

    C. $\frac{1}{20}$

    D. 20

6. A recipe needs 2 teaspoons of black pepper and $\frac{1}{4}$ teaspoon of red pepper. How much more black pepper than red pepper does the recipe need?

    A. $\frac{3}{4}$ of a teaspoon

    B. $\frac{6}{4}$ of a teaspoon

    C. $\frac{3}{2}$ of a teaspoon

    D. $\frac{7}{4}$ of a teaspoon

7. Three times a number is equal to 102. What is the number?

    A. 26
    B. 34
    C. 36
    D. 28

8. Which equation represents this phrase "x decreased by 11"?

   A. 11 – x
   B. x + 11
   C. 11x
   D. x – 11

9. What is the solution of the equation 2y + 8 = 30?

   A. y = 11
   B. y = 13
   C. y = 9
   D. y = 19

10. What is the area of the following rectangle?

    0.5 feet

    7 feet

    A. 7.5 square feet
    B. 6.5 square feet
    C. 35 square feet
    D. 3.5 square feet

11. How many right angles does a square have?

    A. 2
    B. 4
    C. 3
    D. None

12. What figure will this net make?

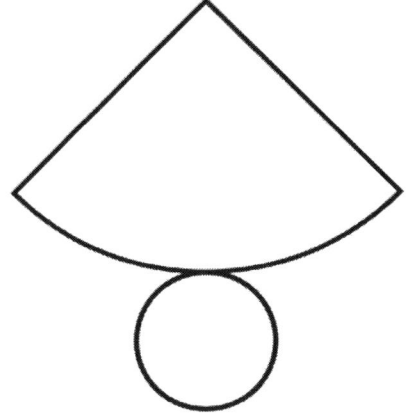

    A. Cylinder
    B. Cone
    C. Sphere
    D. Cube

13. What is the temperature shown on the thermometer?

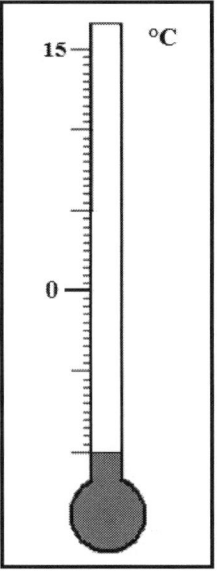

A. −10°C
B. 10°C
C. −5° C
D. There is not enough information given.

14. What time is it?

A. 12:55
B. 11:00
C. 12:11
D. 11:55

15. How many feet are in 4 miles?

    A. 7,040
    B. 253,440
    C. 21,120
    D. 20,140

16. How many quarts are in 180 pints?

    A. 360
    B. 90
    C. 250
    D. 45

17. What is the average of this data set?

    $$8, 11, 22, 19, 5$$

    A. 13
    B. 22
    C. 11
    D. 15

18. The measurement for the center of a distribution is the:

    A. Mode
    B. Range
    C. Sample
    D. Average

19. What is the range of this data set?

    $$19, 7, 22, 45, 66, 32, 21, 8, 9, 54, 16, 18$$

    A. 66
    B. 59
    C. 8
    D. 32

20. The result of $4 - \frac{10}{5}$ is:

　A. $\frac{2}{5}$

　B. 2

　C. $\frac{8}{5}$

　D. 3

21. The result of 200 x 0,8 is:

　A. 160
　B. 16
　C. 1,60
　D. 16,60

22. Jose divided 9 liters of lemonade evenly among some smaller bottles. He put $\frac{3}{4}$ of a liter into each bottle. How many smaller bottles did Jose fill?

　A. 6
　B. 10
　C. 12
　D. 14

23. The fraction $\frac{36}{9}$ can be written as:

　A. 5

　B. $\frac{2}{3}$

　C. $\frac{18}{4}$

　D. 4

24. The result of 42 x $\frac{1}{2}$ is:

　A. $\frac{1}{84}$

　B. 21

　C. $\frac{1}{21}$

　D. 84

25. Which algebraic expression represents the phrase "the quotient of *m* and 17"?

　A. $\frac{17}{m}$

　B. $\frac{m}{17}$

　C. $17m$

　D. $m + 17$

26. Which equation represents the phrase "Twenty dollars was $\frac{1}{3}$ of the total money spent"?

　A. $\frac{1}{3} + x = 20$

　B. $x - \frac{1}{3} = 20$

　C. $\frac{1}{3}x = 20$

　D. $20x = \frac{1}{3}$

27. The solution of the equation $10x + 10 = 90$ is:

　A. x = 10
　B. x = 12
　C. x = 9
　D. x = 8

28. Helen drew 5 quadrilaterals. How many sides did Helen draw?

   A. 5
   B. 15
   C. 30
   D. 20

29. What figure will this net make?

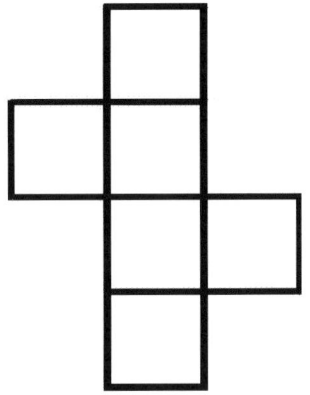

   A. Rectangular prism
   B. Cube
   C. Square pyramid
   D. Cylinder

30. How many corners does a square pyramid have?

   A. 5
   B. 4
   C. 6
   D. 2

31. How many pounds are in 5 tons?

   A. 10,000
   B. 100,000
   C. 1,000
   D. 200,000

32. The building is about 24 feet tall. About how tall is the tree?

   A. 4 feet
   B. 12 feet
   C. 8 feet
   D. 5 feet

33. Which one of the following units is correct for area?

   A. Feet
   B. Gallons
   C. Square inches
   D. Inches

34. Which one of the following is true?

   A. 2 yards = 8 feet
   B. 160 ounces = 16 pounds
   C. 1 meter = 1,000 centimeters
   D. 8 quarts = 2 gallons

35. The average of 4, 8, x, and 12 is 7. What is x?

   A. 7
   B. 6
   C. 10
   D. 8

36. What is the median of the following data set?

    50, 200, 500, 400, 100

    A. 500
    B. 200
    C. 50
    D. 100

37. Which point has the coordinates (2, 0)?

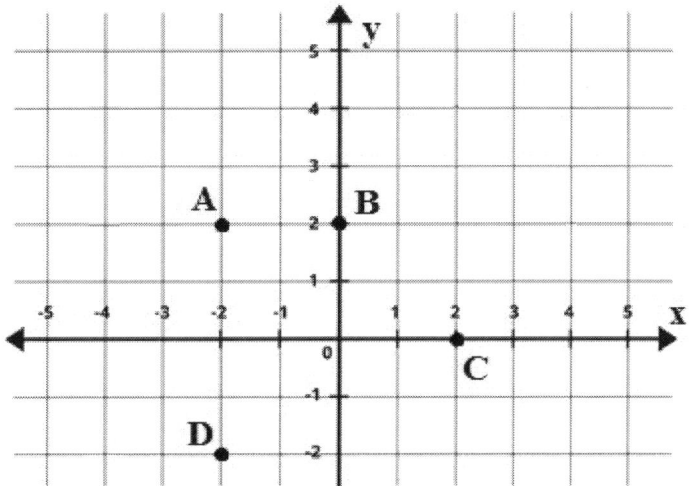

    A. Point B
    B. Point A
    C. Point D
    D. Point C

38. Which of the following is the smaller unit of linear measurement?

    A. Kilometer
    B. Centimeter
    C. Meter
    D. Millimeter

39. The result of $\frac{10}{2} + \frac{20}{4}$ is:

    A. 10

    B. $\frac{30}{6}$

    C. 5

    D. $\frac{30}{4}$

40. Which of the following is an equation?

    A. 2x – 3y
    B. 10a
    C. 56 + z
    D. b + 6 = 16

Reflection on Practice Test # 2

Answer the following reflection questions and feel free to discuss your responses with your teacher or a classmate.

1- How do you feel about your performance on the practice test?

2- Was anything too hard for you? What was it?

3- Was anything too easy for you? What was it?

4- What math procedures do you still need to review?

5- List the math procedures and skills that you need to work on or to practice more.

6- What else do you want your teacher to know?

PRACTICE TEST ANSWER KEYS

PRACTICE TEST #1

1 - c	9 - c	17 - a	25 - b	33 - c
2 - d	10 - a	18 - c	26 - c	34 - b
3 - b	11 - d	19 - b	27 - a	35 - a
4 - d	12 - b	20 - d	28 - d	36 - c
5 - a	13 - c	21 - a	29 - b	37 - d
6 - b	14 - b	22 - c	30 - b	38 - c
7 - c	15 - a	23 - b	31 - a	39 - a
8 - d	16 - d	24 - d	32 - d	40 - d

PRACTICE TEST #2

1 - b	9 - a	17 - a	25 - b	33 - c
2 - d	10 - c	18 - d	26 - a	34 - d
3 - a	11 - b	19 - b	27 - c	35 - a
4 - c	12 - b	20 - b	28 - d	36 - b
5 - a	13 - a	21 - a	29 - b	37 - d
6 - c	14 - d	22 - c	30 - a	38 - d
7 - b	15 - c	23 - d	31 - a	39 - a
8 - d	16 - b	24 - b	32 - c	40 - d

ABOUT COACHING FOR BETTER LEARNING, LLC

CBL's mission is to develop continuous improvement processes and systems to help individuals and companies increase productivity, reach peak performance, maximize impact, and save time, resources and energy.

Let us know if you have questions at coachingforbetterlearning@gmail.com.

Made in the USA
Monee, IL
15 January 2020